The Biblical Personality

To Bernie and Connie —

with love and joy.

Richard

The Biblical Personality

A RABBINIC ANALYSIS OF HEBREW SCRIPTURE

RICHARD S. CHAPIN

JASON ARONSON INC.
Northvale, New Jersey
Jerusalem

This book was set in 11 pt. Fairfield Light by Alpha Graphics of Pittsfield, NH and print-ed and bound by Book-mart Press, Inc. of North Bergen, NJ.

10 9 8 7 6 5 4 3 2 1

Library of Congress Cataloging-in-Publication Data

Chapin, Richard S.
   The biblical personality / Richard S. Chapin.
     p. cm.
   Includes bibliographical references and index.
   ISBN 0-7657-6033-9
   1. Bible. O.T. Biography. I. Title.
BS571b.C38 1999
221.9'22—dc21
[B]   99-39968
                                              CIP

Printed in the United States of America on acid–free paper. For information and cata-log write to Jason Aronson Inc., 230 Livingston Street, Northvale, NJ 07647-1726, or visit our website: www.aronson.com

To Harold Chapin (*z"l*)
ish tzadik tamim hayah bedorotav
"a righteous man, perfect in his generations." (Gen. 6:9)

Contents

༄

Acknowledgments

Υears of Torah study, years of collegial support; the two go hand in hand. I have been more than lucky in my rabbinical career to have had the opportunity to serve at Congregation Emanu-El of New York. I have been even luckier to have received the rabbinical support of our Senior Rabbi, Dr. Ronald B. Sobel, my fellow Associate Rabbis, David M. Posner and Amy Ehrlich, and the friendship of our Cantor, Howard Nevison. Together and individually we strive to fulfill the time-honored role of *mesharet*— serving our congregants, our community, and the Jewish world. The demands upon our time notwithstanding, we have been able to engage in substantive discussions of our religious and intellectual natures. Recognizing our differences, we have continued to appreciate the goodness that is contained within each other. The contributions of my colleagues to this work cannot be overstated; we have engaged in the revered Jewish practice of *shakla v'tarya* for nearly a generation.

The Biblical Personality is, in a slightly different and elongated form, a collection of pieces written for our temple *Bulletin* from the fall of 1996 to the spring of 1998. Our administrative office, led by Dr. Mark W. Weisstuch and assisted by Mark Heutlinger and secretarial personnel, helps produce the temple's *Bulletin*, a weekly publication of which we are rightly proud. During his entire career at our congregation, Steven Mugan has prepared these weekly parcels for mailing. *The Biblical Personality* began as an idea for the *Bulletin*, a vehicle to teach Torah to our people in a concise and pithy manner.

In that regard, I am extremely grateful for the opportunity to employ a scholarly anthology compiled by Rabbi Yisrael Yitzchak Chasidah, *Ishei HaTanach* (1964). Translated and published by the Shaar Press in 1994, it is distributed by Mesorah Publications. This collection, now entitled *Encyclopedia of Biblical Personalities*, has provided a fertile ground of ideas for each personality included in this volume.

Personal thanks are extended to the secretarial staff of the rabbis—Roberta Greenberg, Sandy Herz, and Estelle Hendrickson—who have helped the rabbinate retain a healthy focus in our lives. Estelle Hendrickson deserves particular attention for her formation of the *Bulletin* series, and her attention to the many details of this manuscript. To her goes my most heartfelt gratitude.

Personal thanks are also extended to our congregants, who continue to respond to the ideas, sermons, and classes offered by the rabbinate. The conversation has been pleasant and stimulating for nearly a generation and has inspired many of the thoughts contained within *The Biblical Personality*.

꒜

Introduction

$\mathcal{W}$hereas the familial reading of the Bible was once a staple in American homes throughout the 1800s, in the twentieth century the study and interpretation of Scriptures have been relegated to the synagogue. As a result of this change, the stories and personalities of the biblical characters, even if regularly pursued through the study of the Sabbath lections, have become less familiar to our people and, sadly, forgotten or viewed as traditional relics—on display and accessible to the human eye, but lacking real form and substance.

This situation is more than unfortunate. The ideas and principles contained within the pages of the Bible have always been considered the basis of civilized living. Those of us who value classical literature know that the religious and moral motifs therein have informed every age of humankind. The understanding of nearly all respective disciplines—history, philosophy, psychology, literature, science—requires a sound grounding in biblical thought. Further, the Bible stands alone not only as the ultimate code for our moral behavior, but as a sourcebook of personalities who have served as paradigms for scholars and authors as diverse as Albert Schweitzer, Sigmund Freud, and Herman Melville. Its near disappearance as a referent to the wisdom of the ancient world is a tragedy in the making. It is our people's responsibility to uphold its singular place in our practice of Judaism.

There are countless ways to approach the biblical text. Like exploring the vastness of the African continent, there are so many perspectives that to grasp the Bible's intrinsic meaning can seem quite elusive. Its history, morality, legality, narratives, Hebraic essence, and Divine origin are all subjects that have occupied scholars throughout the ages. Of all these possibilities, perhaps the most vivid and accessible illustrations of Jewish thought may be found in the stories of the Bible and, specifically, in the personalities presented in those stories. These personalities not only come to life in the biblical narrative but remain alive for each generation of readers properly trained to examine them.

Indeed, this is, as the Greeks asserted, *Ho Biblos* (*The Book*), God's gift to the Jewish people, who pledged to honor, maintain, observe, and transmit its contents to an unending succession of generations. And it is the reactions and dialogue of God's creations—from the first respiration of Adam to the last breath of Moses and from the period of the Prophets to Israel's return from exile—that inform and illuminate each precious verse of Torah. The Torah is not only *The Book* but also Judaism's most essential source of religious teaching.

I propose to examine the dramatis personae of *The Book* and hope to bring to light its inner wisdom through a study of the personalities of the biblical text.

꒜

Adam

The fleshy part of Adam's heel outshone the globe of the sun.

(Zohar 1:142b)

When the Holy One, Blessed be He, was about to create Adam, the Attribute of Kindness said: "Let him be created," but the Attribute of Truth said, "Let him not be created." God took Truth and cast it to the ground. Said the ministering angels before the Holy One, "Why do you scorn Truth?" While the ministering angels were debating the issue, The Holy One created Adam.

(Bereishit Rabbah 8:5)

꒜

*E*ven at the beginning of God's creation there was complexity. As Tradition, which knows no bounds of history or time, tells us, Adam, who was brought from the earth (*adamah*) on Rosh Hashanah, was the most precious of all God's creatures. He was closer to God than the ministering angels, closer spiritually and closer physically than all succeeding human creations. A midrash recounts that Adam's human frame extended from the earth to the sky. However, after he and Eve disobeyed the Almighty, the Holy One placed His hands upon Adam and diminished him.

Because of man's indigenous corporeal nature, God would almost surely find fault with Adam and all his progeny. Yet the quest for spiritual and religious perfection, despite the impossibility of its achievement, was injected into the first pages of the biblical narrative. And yet even that noble, if unachievable, idea was already mitigated by another idea set forth in a parable from the midrash cited above—that man's very existence is founded upon the tomb in which Truth is imprisoned. The first man owed his existence to God's mercy. The message? One must sacrifice veracity for the sake of love and compassion.

The counterpart to this is man's search, employing all his God-given intelligence and perception, for the truth, despite living in a world of falsehood. Indeed, no other human being in history received a harsher lesson than Adam. He was expelled from Paradise and descended into the baseness of the world, knowing the good and the evil, purity and sin, the compassion and the cruelty that resided in each human being. Adam had walked in both worlds, he knew the reality of both heaven and earth, and he created for all civilization a paradigm for human behavior. Human beings are surely the crown of God's creation. Yet their very existence, their experience of the pull toward earthly as well as heavenly pleasures, has been beset with as much hardship, anxiety, and guilt as with discernment, love, and blessing. To perceive the goodness of creation but not to perceive the inherent difficulty of the human condition from the beginning and at the beginning of the biblical narrative would be to oversimplify the intent of the Bible, which always recognized our tendency to fall to earth each time we try to ascend heavenward.

~~

Eve

At first the intention was to create two separate people, but in the end Adam and Eve were created as one for God saw that only through this could there be peace between people. First to be cursed was the serpent, thereafter Eve, and finally Adam.

(*Eruvin* 18a)

~~

*I*n the fifth chapter of the book of Genesis the text states, "Male and female He created them." Yet in the first chapter of Genesis it is written, "God created man in His image." This textual incongruity is explained by the talmudic sages as the difference between Divinity's intent and His actual creation. God intended to create two human beings but ultimately created one. It is no small distinction, and an examination of what seem to be two separate creation narratives has offered theologians an infinite number of problems and resolutions throughout history.

Taken as mythos, the story of man and woman's creation may be seen as a giant fairy tale, an ancient fiction symbolizing the beginning of human tenure on earth. Taken as a religious truth, the co-creation of Adam and Eve points to the difficulties, anxieties, and sinful nature that inured within God's first creatures, from the very moment of their existence.

Who was Eve? The Hebrew, *Chava*, means "life-giver," which has literal truth, since Eve nursed the whole world. But *Chava*, in its Aramaic form, also denotes a serpent and, indeed, a serpent enticed the first female. It is this image that has been sustained throughout history: the seduction of Eve, which led to both her and Adam's fall from grace and expulsion from the Garden. And yet Adam and Eve's fates were inextricably intertwined. As one creation, neither could fully blame the other for sinning; indeed, as God either knew or would soon learn, disobeying the word of the Lord was as indigenous to the human condition as Adam and Eve's physical forms. After Eve gave Adam the forbidden fruit, the eyes of *both* of them were opened, and they realized that they were naked.

Giving up the earthly paradise, though tragic, was ultimately what distinguished Adam and Eve from all the other creatures. By eating of the Tree of Knowledge Eve inadvertently displayed the independence of thought that would characterize human behavior from that moment onward. Woman and man could now discriminate between good and bad, a quality not possessed by cattle and beast. At the same time, if man and woman were to eat from the Tree of Knowledge and obtain earthly immortality, they might spend all their days pursuing gratification instead of developing their spirits and performing good deeds. Thus Eve, who preceded Adam in knowledge of good and evil, shared with her co-creation the fate of all humanity to follow: to live and die in pursuit of knowledge and the good and the avoidance of evil. As in the case of our historic first couple, the result has been a mixed blessing.

＊

Cain

Cain did not resemble Adam, and his descendants are not listed in the account of Adam's descendants.

(see Gen. 5:1; *Targum Yonatan, Bereishit* 42)

Cain said to Abel, "There is no justice, no judge, no World to Come, and no reward and punishment for the righteous and the wicked." Abel replied: "There is indeed justice, a judge, a World to Come, and reward and punishment." They argued this matter in the field. Then Cain rose up against his brother Abel, hit him in the forehead with a rock, and killed him."

(*Targum Yonatan, Bereishit* 4:8)

＊

*T*he first book of the Bible opens with Adam's sons, Cain and Abel, competing for God's favor, engaging in a fight that leads to the world's first murder. Establishing a pattern of sibling rivalry that is repeated constantly in the biblical text, and most famously in the case of Esau and Jacob, the offering of the younger son, Abel, is preferred to that of his elder brother, Cain.

The text does not tell us why Abel's offering of the firstlings of his flock is more palatable to the Lord than Cain's gift of fruit from the soil. We do learn that Cain is distraught as the Almighty, speaking as intimately as a parent, counsels him and suggests, "Why art thou wroth and why is thy countenance fallen? If thou doest well, shall it not be lifted up? and if thou doest not well, sin coucheth at the door; and unto thee is its desire, but thou mayest rule over it" (Gen. 4:6–7).

Apparently Cain could not control his terrestrial desires and his violent temper, adding another dimension of human frailty to God's crown of creation. He seems, even at this earliest stage of human existence, preternaturally cynical. This characteristic is alluded to in the midrash cited above. Cain feels bereft of God's benevolence. He feels cheated and unrewarded for his labors and jealously confronts his favored brother. Abel retorts, "There is no favoritism in Divine judgment. It is because my deeds are better than yours that my offering has been accepted" (*Targum Yonatan*, Gen. 4:8). It is the bare honesty of Abel's statement that strips Cain of his inner defenses. No longer able to believe in the goodness and justice of the world, he commits the greatest sin since the creation of the world. Like his parents who were exiled from the Garden of Eden, but even more similar to the narrative of Ishmael, he becomes an outcast, an untouchable, disqualified from the genealogical tree of Adam and Eve.

Indeed, Cain is marked by God with a "sign," as he settles east of Eden in the land of Nod. The first child of the first couple receives the Lord's harshest penalties. Cain is to earn his livelihood from the blood-soaked ground, which the Lord will not fertilize. He will remain throughout his earthly existence both a fugitive and a wanderer. In this case, and in many biblical accounts to follow, Cain's guilt and punishment literally fit the crime.

Methuselah

"And all the days of Methuselah were nine hundred sixty and nine years."
(Gen. 5:27)

As long as Methuselah lived, the Flood did not come upon the world. And when Methuselah died, it was withheld for another seven days after his death to fulfill the period of mourning.

(*Avot d'Rabbi Natan* 32:1)

The line of Adam is traced through his third son, Seth. Adam lived 930 years; Seth lived 912. But this was not unusual. These antediluvian years were characterized by great longevity. Methuselah lived the longest of any of the biblical personalities. This was ensured by the biblical dictum, "My spirit shall not abide in man for ever, for that he also is flesh; therefore shall his days be a hundred and twenty years."

(Gen. 6:3)

What earned Methuselah, Noah's grandfather, the title of the world's "oldest man"? There are no hints in the biblical text. However, the rabbinical literature exalts him: "Methuselah was perfectly righteous. Whatever came out of his mouth ended with the praise of the Holy One, Blessed is He. He studied 900 orders of Mishnah."

(*Yalkut Shimoni, Bereishit* 42)

ᴣᴖ

$\mathcal{T}$he Talmud identifies the "seven shepherds" from the messianic vision of Micah as, "David in the center with Adam, Seth, and Methuselah on his right, and Abraham, Jacob, and Moses on his left" (*Sukkah* 52b). Further, when Methuselah died, not only did the angels eulogize him in heaven, but God delayed the punishment of the generation of the Flood for the seven days of bereavement.

All the preceding sources suggest that Methuselah was a *tzaddik*, a righteous man, and by implication, a more righteous man than his grandson, Noah. Although Noah was called "righteous and whole-hearted," his righteousness is mitigated by the words "in his generations." Noah is exalted within a debased period of human civilization. Methuselah is and remains exalted in generations inhabited by great men. Thus his goodness and righteousness will always stand at the highest level of both human aspirations and Divine expectations.

He lived nearly a millennium, and his son, Lamech, begot Noah, who was to rescue humanity from degradation and its virtual destruction. Only after Methuselah did the Lord perceive man as corrupt, and perhaps not worth saving. It was the life of Methuselah and his forebears, extending back in time through Seth and Adam, that encouraged Divinity to give his earthly creations a chance to start over. The Lord Himself would soon recognize that the quality of corruption, as much as the quality of goodness, adhered to every human soul succeeding Noah.

Noah

Noah was a scholar who understood the languages of all creatures.

(Zohar Chadash 22b)

"Noah was a righteous man, perfect in his generations" (Gen. 6:9). In his generations he was considered righteous, but he would not have been considered righteous in other generations. Resh Lakish said, "In his generations he was righteous, and surely he would have been righteous in other generations."

(Sanhedrin 108a)

Who was Noah? The question is not easily answered without an understanding of biblical thought and the rabbis who later interpreted the Divine text. At first glance, Noah appears to be a hero, even an early Dr. Doolittle, who saves his generation, produces a new civilization and, through his offspring, new peoples. Scratching the surface, however, one derives, as early as the sixth chapter of Genesis, another biblical principle: not every leader of our people led on the same level. That is, although Noah was considered "righteous and perfect in his generations," he was never considered the equal of Abraham or Jacob or Moses. A midrash underscores this. When God wanted to destroy the Jews after the sin of the golden calf and promised Moses to bring forth a nation from him alone, Moses immediately replied, "Shall I abandon Israel's cause for my personal benefit?" But when God told Noah He would save him in the ark, Noah did not pray for the people of the world, and they perished.

(Zohar 1:67b)

Yet another principle may be derived from this narrative. Although the talents and personal gifts of Israel's leaders most certainly varied throughout the biblical period, the idea is unquestionably set forth that the history of humanity, man's technological and intellectual advancements notwithstanding, was already on a downward slope in God's eyes. This depressing thought is confirmed in the sentence wherein the Lord expanded the menu of humanity to include meat. "Every moving thing that liveth shall be for food for you" (Gen. 9:3). At the same time that man was allowed to eat meat, he was also to inspire fear among God's bestial creatures. "And the fear of you and the dread of you shall be upon every beast of the earth, and upon every fowl of the air, and upon all the fishes of the sea."

(Gen. 9:2)

A new covenant is made with Noah as the Lord causes a rainbow to be seen in the clouds. God promises never to destroy humanity again, yet subsequent events taint the colorful mood of optimism. Noah plants a vineyard and becomes drunk. Noah's child, Ham, the father of Canaan, sees Noah's nakedness and receives an angry curse: "A servant of servants shall he be unto his brethren" (Gen. 9:25). Ham's brothers, Shem and Japheth, are concomitantly blessed. Family *tsuris* (troubles) will bring forth generational conflict. Noah has his rightful place in Israel's history, but it is a sobering thought to recognize that it is hardly at the top rung of Jacob's ladder.

Shem, Ham, Japheth

Japheth was the eldest of his brothers, but Scripture lists them in the order of their wisdom rather than their ages: Shem, Ham, and Japheth.

(*Sanhedrin* 69b)

The sacred books of Scripture may be written, in addition to Hebrew, *only* in Greek because it is written, "May God grant beauty to Japheth, and it will dwell in the tents of Shem" (Gen. 9:27). The beauty of Japheth, that is, the Greek language, shall be in the tents of Shem.

(*Megillah* 9b)

"Ham, the father of Canaan, saw his father's (Noah's) nakedness and told his two brothers" (Gen. 9:22). Ham ridiculed his father's nakedness.

(*Lekach Tov, Bereishit* 9)

*I*t is not always true that the deeds of the righteous are duplicated by their offspring. Genesis 6:1 asserts: "Noah was a righteous man, perfect in his generations." He begot Shem, Ham, and Japheth, who are remembered in a descending order of righteousness. From their loins came the seventy nations. Shem continued the Hebrew line; Japheth, the Greek peoples; Ham, the Ethiopians, Egyptians, and Canaanites. In the eyes of the biblical text, last is most certainly least. Ham is cursed by Noah for mocking his father's drunken stupor as well as his nakedness. His fate, as well as the fate of his national successors, is to serve as the lowliest of slaves.

Japheth has a much happier destiny. The rabbis of late antiquity were infatuated with the Greeks, with both their worldliness and their intellectual perspective. They were stopped from total cultural assimilation by one major, and insurmountable, distinction described succinctly by Rabbi Emil Hirsch: "The Greeks worshiped the holiness of beauty; the Jews worshiped the beauty of holiness."[1] Noah's curse of Ham is followed by blessing Shem and Japheth. As his Hebraic name indicates, Japheth is blessed with beauty and sensitivity. This blessing takes root in ancient Greece and all its vibrant culture. Shem's blessing rests on the future of Israel and its performance of the commandments.

Ultimately, the biblical text subjugates Japheth to Shem. "May God enlarge Japheth, but he will dwell in the tents of Shem" (Gen. 9:27). Japheth's appreciation of beauty is deeply significant, but only if it is placed at the service of the spiritual truths represented by Shem. A life lived strictly in pursuit of the aesthetic, therefore, diminishes man, makes him a victim of his passions. This deifies human beings instead of God. Thus the text merges the characters and characteristics of Shem and Japheth. Shem's blessing of holiness and awareness of Divine presence combines with Japheth's intellectual and physical acuity. Together they are the perfection Noah envisioned in the new world; separate they are the tragedy that afflicts all humanity.[2] The paradigm remains today, sadly unfulfilled.

---

1. E. G. Hirsch sermon quoted in Ginzberg, L. (1928). *Students, Scholars and Saints*, Philadelphia, Jewish Publication Society, p. 7.

2. *The Chumash* (1993). The Stone Edition. Brooklyn, Mesorah Publications, p. 45.

Terah

Terah was a stargazer. He saw in the stars that Haran would be burned and that from Abraham the world would be filled.

(Shocher Tov 9:7)

Terah chose the land of Israel even before the Lord commanded Abraham to go there.

(Midrash HaGadol, Bereishit 11:27)

Terah has a share in the World to Come.

(Bereishit Rabbah 38:12)

*I*t is not true that each of us receives an equal measure of the Divine inheritance. Often, in biblical narrative, the deeds of the children eclipse those of their parents. Perhaps no character casts a greater shadow over his patrimony than Abraham who, according to the rabbinical literature, rejects his father's idolatrous ways in favor of belief in one supreme deity. The interpretation of these early chapters of Genesis seems to read "unlike father, like son."

Why the negative "spin" on Terah by the rabbis of late antiquity? Perhaps the paucity of biblical text on Terah compared to the verses and chapters devoted to Abraham's career is viewed as pejorative. Indeed, the creation of a paternal idolator makes

Abraham's "conversion" even more vivid. The *mise en scène* of Abraham smashing the carved figures in his father's workshop is embedded in every religious school child's mind at an early age. Yet Abraham's rebelliousness is not exactly a prelude to *Look Homeward, Angel*. It is a radical act of faith, to be even more radically reenacted when Abraham later attempts to fulfill another of God's precepts by sacrificing his son, Isaac, on a priestly altar.

Terah seems to be as wooden, as incapable of response, as his statues of worship. And yet the rabbis recognize his contribution as they analyze the verse: "Now these are the generations of Terah. Terah begot Abram, Nahor, and Haran; and Haran begot Lot" (Gen. 11:27). Noting the repetition of Terah in the text, the rabbis conclude that this signifies that Abraham's much-maligned father will have a share in the World to Come. But how does an idolator merit such Divine mercy? Like Moses's father-in-law, Jethro, who eventually sees the light projected by his incomparable son-in-law, Terah understands his failings and fully repents.

Terah has a significant place in Israelite history. As father of the father of the Jewish people he provides the forum for Abraham, whose intellectual and moral status is undeniably superior. That Terah ultimately recognizes Abraham's gift of revelation and bows finally to one God is to his lasting credit. In this story the message proclaims, "like son, like father!"

~

Abraham

Abraham was worthy of being created before Adam, but God said, "Perhaps Adam will spoil things by sinning, and there will be no one to set things right. Therefore, I will create Adam first, so that Abraham will come and repair what he spoils."

(*Bereishit Rabbah* 14:6)

He is called "Abram the Hebrew" (Gen. 14:13) because he spoke the Hebrew language.

(*Midrash HaGadol, Bereishit* 14:13)

Abraham's righteousness stands forever. He said, "I will not leave God," and God did not leave him. Abraham did not rely on the words of his father or his teacher.

(*Shocher Tov* 118:11)

The Attribute of Kindness said, "All the days that Abraham was in the world, I did not have to do my work, for Abraham took my place."

(*Sefer HaBahir* 86)

~

*A*ll of us look for paradigms—guiding patterns in our lives. The ultimate exemplar of the characteristics our tradition extols is Abraham. His qualities of righteousness, humility, hospitality, Torah learning, belief in God, prophecy, leadership, and faithfulness are unmatched in the Bible, Moses notwithstanding. Indeed we know Abraham as *avinu*, our father. Moses is "our teacher." Despite our recognizing the enormity of Moses's gifts, he is portrayed in the Bible and the rabbinical writings as more intellectual than paternal and sentimental. These latter qualities adhere more readily to Abraham. Abraham's tent was always open from both sides, to his family, to strangers, to guests. With Moses, it was always a good idea to make an appointment.

The sentimental side of the father of the Jewish people does not diminish his standard of leadership. Abraham fought against his father's idolatry. Heeding God's imperative, he transported all the souls he and Sarah "had made" (Gen. 12:5) in Haran to Canaan. His generalship defeated inimical kings and invading armies. He pleaded to the Lord to spare the evil city of Sodom. He entered a new covenant with the Almighty and Israel through the endurance of an adult circumcision. He displayed the loyalty of a servant by offering to sacrifice his beloved son, Isaac, on an altar. And he sought the dignity of burial for his beloved Sarah by acquiring the cave of Machpelah—the tomb that would be used for Israel's greatest patriarchs and matriarchs.

Through all his accomplishments, Abraham always understood the most intrinsic elements of human existence. Anchored to an acute personal faith, he realized every material success without sacrificing the primacy of his spirit. He was perhaps the first sincerely religious and pious man in our people's history. A midrash tells us that Abraham was greater than Adam, for Abraham humbled himself saying, "I am but dust and ashes" (*Pesikta Rabbati* 7:10). *The Sayings of the Fathers* advises us to emulate Abraham by possessing "a generous eye, a humble spirit, and subdued desires."

Abraham was tried constantly by God, and each time he not only passed the test but grew in strength and wisdom for the next encounter. He is the great exemplar—for facing good and evil, happiness and pain, despair and loving acceptance. *Avraham Avinu*—Abraham, our father.

Sarah

The Holy One, Blessed is He, spoke to all other righteous women through an angel, but to Sarah He spoke through Divine communication.

(*Lekach Tov, Bereishit* 23:1)

All of Egypt was irradiated with her beauty. Rabbi Yitzhak said, "Some very righteous and prominent women are blessed with beauty that resembles that of Eve, but Sarah was *very beautiful* (Gen. 12:14), even more than the image of Eve.

(*Bereishit Rabbah* 40:5)

All the years of Sarah's life a cloud signifying the Divine Presence hovered over her tent, the flaps of the tent were open from both sides, her dough was blessed, and a lamp burned in her abode from one Sabbath eve to the next. When Sarah died, all these ceased, but when Rebecca came, they all returned.

(*Bereishit Rabbah* 60:16)

Sarah was first called Sarai—in Hebrew, "my princess." As her life evolved, and through her partnership with Abraham, she earned a new appellation, Sarah, no longer "my princess" but "princess" to the whole world. Indeed, if Abraham earned the sobriquet "our father," then Sarah most certainly merited the parallel title "our mother."

Although society changes and definitions of words as well as people's roles acquire different meanings and implications, Sarah continues to endure as a model for all Jewish women. This was a person who viewed her marriage and lifework with Abraham as a "team effort," a career of mutual devotion, dedication, and loyalty to the future of their family and their people.

That she was beautiful, inwardly and outwardly, is biblically explicated. That she was fiercely loyal and determined to protect her domain and her rightful place by Abraham's side, despite that couple's inability to procreate, is also vividly expressed in the text. That she was less than gracious to Hagar, with whom Abraham cohabited, and to Ishmael, who was Hagar and Abraham's child, is eminently understandable in the context of her designated role as matriarch of the Jewish people. Filial preferences took place in the biblical world. Although rescued thousands of years later in the fiction of Herman Melville (by another great Jewish matriarch, Rachel), Ishmael was never seen as the rightful heir of Abraham because he was not the progeny of Sarah.

All this is reconciled through the amazing revelation that Sarah would give birth to a son at the age of 90. Abraham is a mere 100, and their laughter at his and Sarah's fortune is impressed upon our people's heritage through the career of Isaac, whose Hebrew name means "laughter." Sarah seems, in the Divine scheme, to have the last laugh, but considering her life's trials and her anxieties concerning Isaac's destiny, her amusement is, at this mature age, most surely sardonic.

≈

Lot

Abraham did four good things for Lot: (1) "Abraham went and Lot went with him" (Gen. 12:4); (2) "Also Lot who went with Abraham had flocks, herds, and tents" (Gen. 13:5); (3) "Abraham brought back his kinsman, Lot, with his possessions" (Gen. 14:16); and (4) God remembered Abraham when he destroyed Sodom and Gomorrah; so he sent Lot from amidst the upheaval."

(Gen. 19:29) (*Bereishit Rabbah* 41:36)

Because Lot practiced hospitality, he merited prophecy and escaped the destruction of Sodom.

(*Otzar HaMidrashim* 37)

"Lot's wife became a pillar of salt" (Gen. 19:26) because she had sinned with salt the night the angels came to Lot.

(*Bereishit Rabbah* 51:5)

≈

*A*braham's nephew Lot seems, throughout the pages of Israel's destiny, a confused and passive figure. Indeed, without the protection of the righteous Abraham, who rescues his nephew on numerous occasions, Lot most certainly would have perished with the evildoers of Sodom and Gomorrah. He is saved from destruction, however, and his story survives as one of the more instructive narratives in the book of Genesis.

Nowhere is Lot perceived, as Noah was earlier, as "righteous in his generations." But he was the son of Abraham's brother, Haran, who died in Ur Kasdim before Abraham and Sarah's great journey to Canaan. Abraham took responsibility for Lot and had compassion for him, despite his nephew's provocative and often immoral behavior, because Haran had been faithful to and supportive of Abraham. But it was not an easy task. Lot, fitting the modern idiom to the biblical text, was "all over the place." He appeared with Abraham and Sarah at the beginning of the journey to Canaan; he accompanied his uncle and aunt to Egypt; and he was given the plain of Jordan upon which to graze his flocks and pitch his tents as far as Sodom.

Ironically, it was in Sodom that Lot, perceiving true evil, became aware of the possibility of goodness. While Uncle Abraham attempted to save that debauched city from Divine destruction, Lot was hospitable to two angels who came to the gate of the city. Taking a chapter from Abraham's book of etiquette, he fed the angels, again without knowledge that one angel had come to destroy Sodom and the other to save Lot and his immediate family. A curious and disturbing scene ensues. The Sodomites angrily intrude upon Lot's graciousness, and Lot offers his daughters to them in order to protect his heavenly guests. Fortunately, the danger is averted, but Lot, his wife, and two daughters flee the doomed city. On the road, despite being commanded by the angel not to look back, Lot's wife (she is forever unnamed) turns around and is instantly salinized.

Lot seeks shelter in his cave with his two daughters, who devise a plan—to "ply our father with wine and lay with him that we may give life to offspring through our father" (Gen. 19:32). The upshot of this experiment? Lot sires two children who become the progenitors of Israel's national adversaries, Moab and Ammon. And yet, despite Lot's degradation, a Divine spark remains hidden, to be rekindled many generations later in Ruth the Moabitess, from whom King David descends. Our ancestors' uneven journey continues.

Hagar

When Pharaoh took Sarah, he wrote into the marriage contract that he was giving his daughter Hagar to her as a handmaid.

(Midrash HaGadol, Bereishit 16:1)

Sarah, Abraham's wife, took Hagar the Egyptian, her handmaid" (Gen. 16:3). She took her with words saying, "Fortunate are you to be united with this holy man."

(Bereishit Rabbah 45:3)

When Hagar parted from Abraham, she worshiped the idols of her father's house. Later she repented fully and bound herself to good deeds, for which her name was changed to Keturah. After this Abraham sent for and remarried her.

(Zohar 1:133b)

*T*he narrative complexity of the Egyptian, and Hagar's place in biblical history cannot be overstated. If Ishmael would become a wanderer—pushed away from his father Abraham and his Israelite inheritance by the jealous Sarah—he came by it naturally, for Hagar, daughter of Pharaoh, and Sarah's maidservant, endured great suffering and heartbreak in her association with the father and mother of the Jewish people.

According to a midrash, Hagar comes to Abraham and Sarah as a gift from Pharaoh, who had been smitten with Sarah's extraordinary beauty. The gift is seen by Judaism's most prominent couple as compensation for their infertility. In a conversation with her husband, Sarah asserts, "See, now, the Lord has restrained me from bearing; consort, now, with my maidservant, perhaps I will be built up through her" (Gen. 16:2). Abraham does, but the ambivalence of Sarah's comment is an ugly portent. Although the story weaves and darts through more prominent events in Israel's history, the thread of Hagar's destiny is tenaciously pulled along the way. Banished into the wilderness by her mistress, Hagar is allowed to return and she gives birth to Ishmael. Some chapters later, fulfilled by the miraculous birth of Isaac, Sarah, the jealous matriarch, summarily dismisses Hagar and Ishmael. A repentant Abraham secretly follows and assures the inconsolable Hagar that Ishmael will become a great nation. What he assures his mistress is not explicated.

However, in the eyes of the rabbinical literature, Hagar is eventually restored to her rightful place in Abraham's family. After Sarah's death, Abraham marries Keturah (a Hebraic pseudonym for Hagar). Hagar was given this name because her deeds had become as beautiful as *ketoret* (incense) and because she had remained chaste (in Aramaic *keturah* means "restrained") from the time she was separated from Abraham. This far less renowned couple gave birth to many children, none of whom would receive similar inheritances as the nation of Israel did. Wronged from the start, and subjected to a culture and family she did not really understand, Hagar emerges from ignominy, a female precursor of Joseph, to obtain her rightful role in the history of our people. Beginning as Pharaoh's daughter, she had became Abraham's second "princess."

჻

Ishmael

Ishmael said to Isaac, "I am greater than you in the fulfillment of the precepts, for you were circumcised at the age of eight days when you could not protest, whereas I was circumcised at the age of thirteen years when I could have protested."

(*Sanhedrin* 89b)

"Isaac and Ishmael, Abraham's sons, buried him in the cave of Machpelah" (Gen. 25:9). Here Ishmael, the son of the maidservant Hagar, showed honor to Isaac, the son of Sarah, by giving him precedence.

(*Bereishit Rabbah* 62:3)

Because Abraham did not want to bless Ishmael, he did not bless Isaac either, so that Ishmael would not harbor resentment against Isaac.

(*Targum Yonatan, Bereishit* 25:11)

჻

A particularly endearing characteristic of the biblical text and its accompanying rabbinical commentaries is the constant evaluation of great personalities coursing through the scriptural narrative. No character is totally unblemished and no person was considered unredeemable. However, each dramatis persona did acquire a reputation and, through years of reading and interpreting the text, moral judgments were assuredly rendered.

Ishmael, son of Abraham and Sarah's maidservant Hagar, may be the paradigmatic case in point. Notwithstanding his underdog status, there seems to be little sympathy for his biblical exploits. Banned from the tent of the matriarch Sarah, who finds Hagar haughty and disrespectful, the young Ishmael is torn away from his father Abraham, the kindest of all biblical figures, and faces a life and a destiny defined by pangs of abandonment and wanderlust. This was Divinely prefigured. Pregnant with Abraham's firstborn, Hagar learns that although Ishmael is so named because "God has heard" her affliction, the disfavored boy would be "a wild ass of a man—his hand shall be against every man, and every man's hand against him" (Gen. 16:12).

In an age of psychological discourse, it is easy to see why Ishmael was jealous and resented Isaac. It may be harder to understand what effected their eventual reunion, particularly as the biblical text reveals that it was Ishmael who returned from the middle of the desert without enmity and rancor (unlike his nephew Esau, who openly reviled and threatened his brother Jacob) to attend his father's funeral and to defer to his brother Isaac at the burial.

The answer may be found in the goodness that was embodied in Isaac and Ishmael's father, Abraham. Abraham is careful to assure Hagar and Ishmael that he would continue to dower both of them with his spousal and paternal blessings. After Sarah's death, Hagar is rewarded for her faithfulness by acquiring a new name, Keturah, and a happy future with her beloved benefactor in the form of more progeny. Simultaneously, Abraham watches over his exiled son and provides a wife (called Fatimah in the midrash), who is hospitable and kindly in the mode of her exemplary father-in-law, so that Ishmael knows that his father still loves him. That paternal love, and filial reciprocation, underlay the peaceful fraternal reconciliation at Abraham's death. Ishmael's miscreancy is not forgiven, but the redemption of his character cannot be ignored.

ᘿ

Isaac

The Lord said, "I am grateful to Abraham, Isaac, and Jacob, who were the first to make Me known in the world."

(*Menachot* 53a)

When Isaac was bound on the altar, he was 37-years-old.

(*Seder Olam Rabbah* 1)

"The lamb for the offering, my son" (Gen. 22:8). Abraham told Isaac, "You are the lamb."

(*Midrash HaGadol, Bereishit* 22:3)

When Isaac saw Rebecca separate the dough offering in purity, "she became his wife."

(Gen. 24:67) (*Bereishit Rabbah* 60:16)

"Blow the ram's horn before Me on Rosh Hashanah so that I will remember to your credit the binding of Isaac, son of Abraham."

(*Rosh Hashanah* 16a)

Why didn't Abraham bless Isaac? Because he saw in Isaac that Esau would issue from him.

(*Pesikta d'Rav Kahana* 31)

ᘿ

*H*e was named Isaac because his mother, Sarah, laughed when God told Abraham of the impending birth of a son. It was a laugh that resounded through religious history, for Isaac's life served as a paradigm for the life of the Christian savior. Not a little disbelief surrounded the announcement of Jesus's birth as well. According to the Gospel of Matthew, Jesus also descended from the loins of Abraham. Add the picture of Isaac, carrying wood, walking behind his father toward the sacrificial altar and a "lamb" mercifully replacing the 37-year-old "lad" before Abraham can execute His will, and the connection of the two testament figures becomes more tenable. Isaac acts the part of the lamb; Jesus is the lamb's fulfillment.

Isaac never quite measures up to the deeds or personality of his father. This is not necessarily a pejorative. Isaac is still considered one of the patriarchs and remains part of our daily liturgy that honors the God of Abraham, Isaac, and Jacob. But aside from redigging the wells once dug by his father in Gerar, Isaac remains a passive figure. It is Abraham who actively pursues the destiny of Israel, through national and familial conflict and resolution. Isaac is more contemplative. Things happen to him, at least in part, because he cannot seem to get out of the way.

The effect is cumulative. Beginning with the sibling rivalry with Ishmael and the infamous "trial" on Mount Moriah and death of his mother, Isaac seems directionless. Fortunately, Rebecca enters his life, and she is not afraid to make decisions. Unfortunately, some of those decisions lead to further family strife. In Rebecca's most nefarious scheme, Isaac is duped and inadvertently awards Jacob the elder son's blessing, depriving the sullen Esau of the birthright. The two sons of this ambivalent father become mortal enemies, bringing sadness to Isaac who, frail and blind at the end of his life, must have wondered what all the laughter was about that heralded his creation.

꒰

Rebecca

Before the Holy One caused Sarah's sun to set, he caused Rebecca's sun to rise.

(Bereishit Rabbah 58:2)

As long as Sarah was alive, a cloud signifying the Divine Presence was tied to the entrance of her tent. The doors were open wide, her dough was blessed, and a lamp burned in the tent from one Sabbath eve to the next. When she died, all these ceased, but when Rebecca came, they all returned. When Isaac saw Rebecca separate dough in purity, "she became his wife."

(Gen. 24:67) *(Bereishit Rabbah* 60:16)

Rebecca was worthy of bearing the twelve tribal ancestors.

(Bereishit Rabbah 63:6)

She came from Abraham's country, from his kindred, and from his father's house. Eliezer, Abraham's servant, met Rebecca at the well and she provided water for him and his camels, evincing both her remarkable physical beauty and gifts of loving kindness. This meeting was a combination of *bashert* (destiny) and familial manipulation (a *shiddoch*). She left her father's house, the first bride-to-be in Jewish history to receive a veil (the custom of *bedeken*) and the accompanying blessing, "Our sister, be thou the mother of thousands of ten thousands. . . ." (Gen. 24:60). From a distance she saw her intended, the pensive and incomplete Isaac, praying in the field for comfort and consolation. "And Isaac brought her into his mother Sarah's tent, and took Rebecca, and she became his wife; and he loved her. And Isaac was comforted for his mother."

(Gen. 24:67)

ॐ

Surely the anxieties of Isaac's formative years made him a worthy candidate for the psychiatrist's couch. If Joseph was to become the Master of Dreams, Isaac was surely the Master of Ambivalence. Yet Rebecca's strength of purpose resolved any lack of resolve that ever plagued this frailest of patriarchs. Rebecca, however, continued to grow in stature and in dominion, and it was her hand that determined her family's destiny as she literally "pulled the wool" over the blind and enfeebled Isaac in order to ensure the hegemony of the "chosen son" Jacob.

These were simultaneously great and tortuous days, when the Jewish people was still young. Family destiny became national destiny, and a bit of subterfuge left one child eternally enshrined among the heroes of our tradition and another child eternally fighting for recognition. Did Rebecca unduly influence the fate of her twin boys? If so, she was only being faithful to the Almighty, who in the only biblical verse directed to a woman said to her, "Two nations are in thy womb, and two peoples shall be separated from thy bowels; And the one people shall be stronger than the other people; And the elder shall serve the younger" (Gen. 25:23). Alas, the familial conflict has been canonized. It is our task both to mitigate and to live with it.

~3~

Laban

After Rebecca had given birth to Esau and Jacob, Laban begot two daughters, Leah and Rachel. They exchanged letters and agreed between themselves that Esau would take Leah as a wife and Jacob would take Rachel.
(*Tanchuma, Vayeitzei* 12)

Laban would renege ten times on any agreement he made with Jacob.
(*Bereishit Rabbah* 73:9)

"Jacob told Rachel that he was her father's brother" (Gen. 29:12). He said, "I am his brother in deceit for it is written, 'With the crooked act crookedly.'"
(Ps. 18:27) (*Megillah* 13b)

~3~

*I*n a tradition that holds firmly to the religious principle of redemption, the career of Laban leaves us virtually nonplussed. So creatively manipulative are Laban's familial machinations that the reader of the Bible may errantly conclude that Rebecca's brother only "wanted what was good for his children." This refrain, dusted off and dragged out by every generation that succeeded the untrustworthy Laban, has often achieved the opposite effect, that is, the expression of the most negative feelings between offspring and their parents. Laban's actions are selfishly premeditated. His heart does not aspire to the deeds of his ancestor, Abraham. Indeed, his scientific coldness prefigures the creation of Nathaniel Hawthorne's chilling character, Ethan Brand.

Yet Laban's destiny does not end in a limekiln. He is the father of two redoubtable daughters of Judaism, Leah and Rachel, as well as the father-in-law of one of our tradition's most revered patriarchs, Jacob. If there is guilt by association, so here there must be some redemptive spark in the virtuous offspring of Laban. Can we assume Laban was at least a good father? Or was divinity resting a specific duration before illuminating the next generation with His goodness? Although the latter is more likely, one finds the Laban-Jacob narrative compelling on many levels. Perhaps the most interesting layer is that Jacob learns, in the face of so much deception from his recalcitrant and dishonest father-in-law (who passes off history's first two-for-one bargain), that every interaction between Laban and his son-in-law was simply business as usual. That is, Jacob had to learn that in Laban's world everything was negotiable and for sale, and if he was to succeed in his father-in-law's realm, he would have to be as crafty and as conniving as Laban.

That Jacob succeeded in his venture, with the help of the Almighty, was only natural. He had already disposed of Esau in a mighty and inimical competition involving his mother's encouraging deceitfulness. Jacob spent twenty years in Laban's tents—fourteen years for Leah and Rachel and six years pasturing the flocks. In a memorable chase and confrontation, after Jacob and his family fled from the vengeful Laban, and Rachel stole her father's precious religious idols, the two blood enemies made a pact to leave each other alone. Laban was never appeased, but by this late date, there was no filial guilt. This is the last contact with Mesopotamia and Laban's family. As the star of Mesopotamia faded into the darkness, Israel's destiny brightened.

Jacob

There were three people to whom the Holy One gave a taste of the World to Come while they were yet in this world, and as a result the evil inclination had no power over them. These were Abraham, Isaac, and Jacob.

(*Bava Batra* 17a)

Because he had accepted evil reports from Joseph, the Divine Presence departed from Jacob for twenty-two years.

(*Otzar HaMidrashim* 172)

Thereupon Jacob made this vow: "If God will be with me" (Gen. 28:20). Why didn't Jacob believe God's promise of protection? He thought, "This is a dream, and dreams are sometimes true and sometimes not. If the promise is fulfilled, I will know that the dream was true."

(*Zohar* 1:150b)

"In the morning . . . behold it was Leah" (Gen. 29:25)! Jacob said to her, "Deceiver and daughter of a deceiver! At night I called you Rachel and you responded to that name." She replied, "Is there a school without disciples? Did your father not call you Esau, and did you not respond?"

(*Bereishit Rabbah* 70:19)

He was born holding onto the heel of his elder twin brother, and so was named Jacob, derived from the Hebrew *akev*, meaning heel or supplanter. This fraternal conflict was prefigured. The Lord had informed Rebecca

that "two nations are in thy womb . . . and the elder shall serve the younger"
(Gen. 25:23). Although fratricide was averted, Esau's anger at being supplanted by his more clever and more chosen brother would cause Jacob
anxiety and grief throughout his life. Was it any surprise that near the
end of his life, after Joseph brought him down to Egypt, Jacob would assess
his destiny succinctly and gravely saying, "The days of the years of my
sojourns have been a hundred and thirty years. Few and evil have been
the days of the years of my life, and they have not reached the life spans
of my forefathers in the days of their sojourns."

(Gen. 47:9)

꒰ꕤ꒱

*M*anipulated by his mother, Jacob eventually experiences the
rabbinical principle of *mida keneged mida* (measure for measure)
firsthand. Once he dupes his brother Esau to earn the right of
primogeniture, so too is Jacob later duped by Laban who, ironically, through replacing Rachel in the bridal chamber with Leah,
upholds the custom that Rebecca and Jacob had earlier under-
mined. In the midrash Leah reminds Jacob of this fact, and the
proof of her rightful place in Jacob's family history is the two
children who emanate from their union: Levi, who establishes the
priesthood, and Judah, the progenitor of Israel's kings.

Jacob, the father of the Bible's great dreamer, Joseph, dreams
dreams of his own. His most remarkable dream depicts a ladder
reaching heavenward with angels ascending and descending its
rungs. The Lord appears by Jacob's side and blesses the future
patriarch:

The land whereon thou liest, to thee will I give it, and to thy seed.
. . . And in thee and in thy seed shall all the families of the earth
be blessed. And, behold, I am with thee, and will keep thee whither-
soever thou goest, and will bring thee back into this land; for I will
not leave thee, until I have done that which I have spoken to thee
of. (Gen. 28:13–15)

Jacob awakes, in awe of divinity's promise. Taking a stone he had
used as a pillow, he "set it up for a pillar, and poured oil upon the
top of it. And he called the name of that place Beth-el" (the house
of God) (Gen. 28:18–19).

The return to the land was predicted, but the extended Mesopotamian interlude was not. Finally extracting his family from the clutches of Laban, Jacob confronts his earliest adversary, Esau, in the land of Seir. Dividing his camp into two parts, Jacob, anticipating Esau's wrath, spends a sleepless night alone. Another dream/encounter pits the maturing Jacob wrestling a man/angel who inflicts injury upon the patriarch while bestowing upon him the name Israel because Jacob "had striven with God and prevailed" (Gen. 32:29). Fittingly, the place is called Peniel "for I have seen God face to face, and my life is preserved" (Gen. 32:31). Although Jacob walks away with a limp, he has earned divinity's highest honor. Henceforth the names of the patriarch and the nation—Jacob–Israel—are cojoined. The young "supplanter" is now the progenitor of the twelve tribes.

It is an enormous responsibility, particularly as Jacob endures the next generation's version of fraternal strife between Joseph and his jealous brothers. All this takes its toll on the patriarch who, at the end of his life, is comforted to learn that Joseph is alive, well, and prosperous. Descending to Egypt to visit his successful son, Jacob finally blesses his children, known eponymously as *Benei Yisrael*, literally "the children of Israel," but more correctly as "the Israelites." Instructing his family to bury him in the cave of the patriarchs and matriarchs in the land of Canaan, Jacob "expires and is gathered to his people" (Gen. 49:33).

cᴢᴩ

Esau

"The children agitated within Rebecca" (Gen. 25:22). When Rebecca stood near synagogues and houses of study, Jacob would struggle to come forth; and when she passed by temples of idol worship, Esau would push to come forth.

(*Bereishit Rabbah* 63:6)

"The boar of the forest ravages Israel" (Ps. 80:14). The boar is the wicked Esau.

(*Shocher Tov* 120:6)

Rabbi Shimon ben Gamliel said, "No man ever honored his fathers as I honored my fathers; but I found that Esau honored his father even more than I honored mine."

(*Devarim Rabbah* 1:15)

Just as the Divine name rested upon Jacob, so should it have rested upon Esau. Esau was worthy of producing kings, and Jacob, priests. But all of these gifts were taken away from Esau when he sold his birthright to Jacob.

(*Midrash Shir HaShirim*, ed. Buber 18)

cᴢᴩ

*P*art of attaining maturity is recognizing that no life, no personality, is completely pure and good. We search for paradigms of goodness and purity—first in our families and later in our religious heritage—and learn, if we are discerning, that even our greatest models of existence are flawed and imperfect. Internalizing this, we may as well be inspired to examine its converse: that no life, no personality, is completely impure and evil. This is patent, all the negatory evidence notwithstanding.

Esau is a figure, not unlike Ishmael, who begs for the gentle touch of a loving hand. From birth he received the opposite. Attacked prenatally at the heel by his soon to be more favored twin brother Jacob, he unconsciously develops an Achilles complex, striving to win over his family through the physical arts of war and hunting, rather than through the use of his intellect. Perhaps no narrative in Jewish history better defines the Jewish preference of "brain over brawn" than the Jacob–Esau struggle. The younger brother constantly outstrips his older, more athletic sibling. The contest for parental favor, for filial and national inheritance, is constantly waged by the two. The Greeks called this competition *agon* and, for Esau, the final agony is unfortunately immortalized. His descendants include the greatest enemies of the Jewish people: the evil Amalek, Haman, and the Roman Empire.

And yet there are extremely intimate, loving moments in Esau's life. He was loved by his father, Isaac, for his physical prowess. And he returned that love. The rabbis of the midrash both recognize and expound upon it. And deep down, underlying all the fear and anxiety that surrounded his ultimate meeting with Jacob, Esau was looking for love and, for a change, not "in all the wrong places." At their reunion, despite a lifetime of divergent beliefs and practices, ". . . Esau ran to meet him [Jacob], and embraced him, and fell upon his neck, and kissed him; and they wept" (Gen. 33:4). Dots over every letter of the Hebrew word *vayyishakehu* ("and he kissed him") point to hidden textual allusions. Although it is an immutable rule that Esau hates Jacob, and that everyone hates Esau, the commentator Rashi suggests that this was a moment of merciful sincerity. Esau truly embraced Jacob with all his heart. In the process of evaluating and, perhaps, reevaluating Esau's inimical legacy, might this not be a good verse with which to begin?

‌‌‌ ❧

Leah

After Rebecca bore Esau and Jacob, Laban begot two daughters, Leah and Rachel. Rebecca and Laban exchanged letters and agreed that Esau would marry Leah, and Jacob would marry Rachel. Leah constantly wept over this, and from weeping, "Leah's eyes were tender."
(Gen. 29:17) (*Tanchuma*, ed. Buber, *Vayeitzei* 12)

Who are the "women in the tent" (Judg. 5:24)? They are Sarah, Rebecca, Rachel, and Leah—for they were exceptionally modest in their tents.
(*Maharsha Horiot* 10b)

No one thanked the Holy One Blessed is He, until Leah came and thanked Him. She declared, "This time let me gratefully praise the Lord."
(Gen. 29:35) (*Berachot* 7b)

❧

Jacob, the younger and more clever twin, is used to getting his way. Having overturned the inheritance of Esau, he proceeds confidently to Haran. Meeting Rachel at the famous well, he audaciously kisses her and then asks Laban, his kinsman, for her hand in marriage. But Laban is no easy touch. He exacts a promise from Jacob that will translate into twenty years of servitude. It is a contract quite dependent on the exigencies of the day, particularly when it came to the parceling out of Laban's daughters! Though Jacob desires Rachel, the tender-eyed Leah is substituted on the evening of marital consummation. Technically, Laban acts within the rules, as he reminds the angry Jacob the next morning: "It is not so done in our place, to give the younger before the first born" (Gen. 29:26). It must have been particularly galling for the young patriarch to have been reminded, by his immoral relative, of his earlier manipulation of Esau.

And who is this "tender-eyed" young woman? The rabbis avoid, through clever midrashic treatment, the obvious: that is, Rachel is physically more attractive than her older sister. "Rachel was of beautiful form and fair to look upon" (Gen. 29:17). But Leah has inner strength and inner beauty. She asserts her rights with Jacob in the tent of cohabitation, and despite the fact that Jacob "loved Rachel more than Leah" (Gen. 29:30), the Lord rewards Leah with one half, six, of the eventual twelve tribes of Israel. Again, the message of Torah is remarkably current. The tradition extols women of profound external beauty, particularly those who become matriarchs of our people. Yet there is Divine recognition that one is rewarded for the performance of *mitzvot*, deeds of loving kindness that express a deeper internal loveliness. Of the latter, Leah is most certainly endowed. She is the first person mentioned in the Torah to give thanks to God for allowing her to bear children, naming her fourth son Judah, meaning "praise the Lord."

Leah never lets her physical infirmity take away from her rightful role as one of the four matriarchs of Judaism. Like Sarah, she is "restored" by God, with a little assist from Rachel, to her proper place in her and Jacob's family, which is no less than the wife and mother of Israel.

Rachel

"God remembered Rachel" (Gen. 30:22). He remembered her silence for her sister's sake when Leah was given in marriage to Jacob.

(Bereishit Rabbah 73:4)

The matriarch Rachel was one of the first prophetesses.

(Yerushalmi Berachot 9:3)

"I buried her there on the road" (Gen. 48:7). Jacob told Joseph, "Just as you wish that your mother had been buried in the Cave of Machpelah, so did I wish it." Joseph replied, "If so, give the order now, and I will rebury her there." Jacob responded, "You cannot, my son, for I buried her on the road by Divine command. In the future my children will go into exile. When they pass Rachel's tomb, they will embrace it. She will stand and pray for mercy on their behalf, and the Holy One, Blessed is He, will accept her prayer."

(Pesikta Rabbati 3:60)

*I*t is natural to think of Abraham and Sarah as the father and mother of the Jewish people. They are correctly viewed as the first Jewish couple. Yet Sarah, her greatness notwithstanding, must give way to her later descendant, Rachel, who through her life and particularly through her death and place of burial, became the emotional matrix of Judaism.

She doesn't come from the most noble household. Her father, Laban, is a master of deceit, and it is only natural that she and Leah would be caught up in the wily old Mesopotamian's plan to entrap Jacob into marrying both his daughters. But Rachel prevails, even after she must endure being replaced in the marriage canopy by her older sister. She prevails despite her natural jealousy because she understands her role both in her family and in Jewish history. Unable at first to conceive, Rachel courageously reasons, "If I am not worthy enough to have the Jewish nation descend from me, let it descend from my sister Leah" (*Bereishit Rabbah* 71:2).

But her goodness is rewarded, and although Leah gives birth to one half of the tribes of Israel, Rachel gives birth to Joseph and Benjamin, two especially blessed children. By allowing the less desired Leah the opportunity to fulfill her familial desire with Jacob, Rachel would become the most sympathetic character in the Bible. She is seen, even biblically, as the figure who would understand the suffering of the Jewish people. When the Jews are led into captivity by the Babylonians after the destruction of the First Temple, they pass by Rachel's grave on the road to Bethlehem. There they are Divinely comforted, "A voice is heard in Ramah, lamentation, and bitter weeping, Rachel weeping for her children" (Jer. 31:15). Presently Rachel is reassured by the Lord: "Refrain thy voice from weeping, and thine eyes from tears; for thy work shall be rewarded . . . and they shall come back from the land of the enemy" (Jer. 31:16).

Rachel is the mother to all the Jewish children of every exile. Her fame waxes centuries later in the literary realm of Herman Melville where, at the end of *Moby Dick*, Rachel (now a ship) rescues Abraham's misbegotten son Ishmael. Rachel, our Mother.

Dinah

"And Dinah, the daughter of Leah, went out to see the daughters of the land" (Gen. 34:1) to show the gentiles her beauty, so they would see that there was none like her among them.

(Sechel Tov, Bereishit 34:1)

Dinah conceived and bore Asenath. The sons of Israel wished to kill the child. Instead, the angel Michael brought her down to the house of Potiphera in Egypt. Potiphera's wife raised her like a daughter, and later she married Joseph.

(Pirkei d'Rabbi Eliezer 38)

Job lived during the days of Jacob and married his daughter, Dinah.

(Bava Batra 15b)

*W*hen Dinah, the daughter of Leah, goes out of her family's tent to view the "daughters of the land," she is violated by one of the princes of the region, Shechem the Hivite. It is a distressing tale, as its resolution purports a punishment that fits the initial crime. Outwitting the ingratiating family of Shechem and his father Hamor, who want to be accepted by the Israelites, Jacob's sons require a communal circumcision of the adult males, and

then, during the time of their pain, egregiously slaughter each male
by the sword. Even at this early stage of the patriarchal period, it
is an astonishingly vindictive reprisal. When an angry Jacob chas-
tises his vigilante sons, they answer unflinchingly, "Should he treat
our sister like a harlot" (Gen. 34:31)? Jacob is left speechless.

Poor Dinah seems victimized for mere curiosity. She is called
the "daughter of Leah" because her mother was also outgoing:
"And Jacob came from the field in the evening, and Leah went
out to meet him" (Gen. 30:16). As Leah "went out" so too did
Dinah: "And Dinah the daughter of Leah, whom she had borne
unto Jacob, went out to see the daughters of the land" (Gen. 34:1)
(*Bereishit Rabbah* 80:1). The rabbis view this disregard of modesty as improper for a patriarch's daughter, but this is Dinah's
inheritance. Her pattern of behavior is immortalized in Ezekiel
16:44, which reads: "As the mother, so her daughter." But she is
also called the "daughter of Jacob" because his distinguished reputation, in addition to her great beauty, influences Shechem to
covet her.

Yet tradition rescues Dinah from her ignominy. She is perceived, in the rabbinical literature, as the suffering wife of the
righteous Job, the long-suffering servant of God. If this were not
enough, from the cowardly act of Shechem emerges progeny—
Asenath, who is angelically transported to the Egyptian royal
household and raised by Joseph's Egyptian temptress. Asenath's
fate is a happy one. She assumes the hallowed role of Joseph's
wife. Her children, Ephraim and Manasseh, receive their grandfather Jacob's special blessing, a benediction that is pronounced
over every generation of Jewish children each Sabbath evening.
From dishonor to honor. From humiliation to nobility. Dinah—
through her life and through her offspring—experiences it all.

Joseph

"He was a youth" (Gen. 37:2). He acted like a youth, adorning his eyes, lifting his heels, and combing his hair.

(Bereishit Rabbah 84:7)

On account of a dream he was distanced from his brothers, and on account of a dream he was elevated above his brothers and the entire world.

(Zohar 1:191b)

Throughout the years that the Israelites were in the desert, two arks traveled together—that of the dead (Joseph's coffin) and that of the Ark of the Covenant. When Moses was asked if it was proper for the dead to travel with the Divine Presence he replied, "This one fulfilled all that is written in the other."

(Sotah 13a)

More attention is devoted to Joseph than to any other character in the Genesis narrative. It is a compelling saga that brings to light a person who resembles his forebears. There is by now a biblical pattern of maturation. Immature youth is tested by inimical and corrupting forces; eventually personal and family conflicts are resolved while ascending to a position of exalted patriarch. Joseph follows and achieves this pattern with one significant difference: Joseph is a master of dreams. "Behold, I have dreamed a dream: and, behold, the sun and the moon and eleven stars bowed down to me."

(Gen. 37:9)

ᒥ

 $\mathcal{T}$ he dreams come to him as a youth, and they are youthfully resented by his older brothers, who have reason to resent the favored and narcissistic Joseph, for he is Rachel and Jacob's "additional" son. The problem is that the youth has a mission. He must offend. In this way, Joseph is the prototype of all Israel's prophets to come. He cannot help himself. When the truth is presented before him, he must utter it. This is the source of his effulgence; it is also the basis for all the difficulty and hardship in his life. After being hurled into the pit and sold to the Ishmaelites (who know firsthand about outcasts), he somehow lands in Pharaoh's house with an almost feline precocity. There he continues to dream and speak. He becomes Pharaoh's trusted viceroy and, because of his prescience, preserves the entire nation of Egypt through an unforgiving seven years of famine.

He marries the Egyptian Asenath, whom the midrash identifies as the daughter of Dinah. Literally, it is an intermarriage. But the children (Manasseh and Ephraim) are Jews and their names are invoked in Jacob's blessing, a benediction still employed by Jewish parents every Sabbath evening. There is eventual reunion with apologetic brothers and a weary Jacob. At the end of Genesis, Joseph adjures his brethren to carry his bones out of Egypt at the time of the Exodus. Moses fulfills the prescription, and Joseph receives the ultimate honor, as his coffin accompanies the Ark of the Covenant throughout the forty years in the wilderness.

~

Benjamin

"Joseph's brother Benjamin, the son of his mother."

(Gen. 43:29)

What is meant by "the son of his mother"? Benjamin's countenance resembled that of his mother, Rachel.

(*Zohar* 1:202b)

When Joseph was sold to Egypt, his righteous brother Benjamin took his spiritual place, lest it be missing.

(*Zohar* 1:259a)

"Rachel, as she lay dying, called her newborn son Ben Oni, but his father, Jacob, called him Benjamin."

(Gen. 35:18)

~

W hat's in a name? For Jews, everything. In the throes of childbirth Rachel, knowing her death is imminent, cries out the name Ben Oni, "son of my mourning." It is a clear comment that her second son's birth has caused her death. But Jacob, ever resourceful, makes the most scrupulous emendation. Not wanting to abrogate his beloved wife's last request, he removes the opprobrious connotation of mourning and substitutes the Hebrew word *yamin*, which literally means "right." Thus *Ben-yamin* becomes "son of the right," that is, "son of strength," since the right hand is a symbol of strength and success.

In the Bible, history repeats itself, and the parallels of Benjamin's life to Joseph's are worthy of note. When Joseph, who was loved by his father more than all his brothers, is sold into slavery, Benjamin becomes the most favored son in Jacob's eyes. Benjamin's replacement of Joseph is reminiscent of the sacrifice of Isaac. As Isaac is rescued from the horror of Abraham's knife, and a lamb is substituted for slaughter, so too does Benjamin take Joseph's place. Fortunately for Benjamin, the story does not conclude with his death.

And yet, like Joseph, he is sorely tested. It seems, in examining the elaborate scheme Joseph employs to bring first Benjamin and then his father down to Egypt, that he is exacting vengeance not only upon the guilty brothers, who had sold him into slavery, but also upon the lamblike Benjamin, who had the audacity to replace his older brother as Jacob's favorite son. Joseph couldn't redeem the years he had been bereft of his father's love, but he could exact a price, even upon the brother whose hands and heart were clean.

Fortunately, Judah intervenes, and his intelligent petitions on behalf of Benjamin penetrate Joseph's innermost emotions. Discarding the revenge motif, falling upon Benjamin's neck, kissing and weeping with his brothers, Joseph confesses his identity, his Divine mission, his anguish and abiding love for his family. Jacob can now be informed that it is safe to come down to Egypt.

The reunited family settles in Egypt. Seventeen years later Jacob, near death, blesses his children and grandchildren. Benjamin receives the benediction: "Benjamin is a predatory wolf; in the morning he will devour prey and in the evening he will distribute spoils" (Gen. 49:27). Benjamin's descendants are mighty, fearless warriors—from King Saul to Mordecai and Esther. From timid beginnings to heroic exploits. Benjamin, the "son of strength."

Tamar

The episode of Tamar is read publicly because of the confession of Judah, which is to his credit.

(Megillah 25a)

Judah wanted to pass by Tamar, but the Holy One sent the angel of desire, who said to him, "Judah, where are you going? Whence shall kings and great men arise?" So against his will, "Judah detoured to her by the road." (Gen. 38:16)

ৼ

*I*n the midst of the elongated biblical narrative of Joseph, the reader is confronted with Chapter 38, which is an interpolation often overlooked yet brimming with meaning and import. Here one learns the sordid secrets of Judah's family life, barely a chapter after he has sold his younger brother Joseph into slavery. Beset by guilt, Judah has settled his family in Adullam, thinking he might begin a new chapter and perhaps acquire a new identity and a more noble reputation.

But the biblical narrative, ever conscious of historical precedence as well as just rewards and punishments, plays out an astonishing *mise en scène* that first involves the immediate family but later affects Jewish history. Marrying a woman of the region named Bat Shua, Judah fathers three sons. His first son, Er, marries Tamar but is sentenced to death by the Almighty on account of his evil actions. The second son, Onan, is told to fulfill his leviratic duties by siring children with the widow Tamar. Onan proves unwilling and immature, and the unhappy Tamar is now told by her father-in-law to wait for the third son, Shelah, to grow up and fulfill his responsibilities.

But Tamar has seen enough and senses, as Shelah passes the age of eligibility, that Judah may have reneged on his promise. Covering herself with a veil, she appropriates a place on the road where her father-in-law would pass by. He does and, noting her garb, mistakes her for a harlot. After some inimitable biblical bargaining, they consort. Tamar craftily obtains a tangible pledge from Judah—his signet, his wrap, his staff, and his child-to-be. Three months later Judah is informed of Tamar's harlotry. Enraged, he threatens her life but receives the surprise of his own when she sends him a package of the implicating vestments. Judah, recognizing his own guilt (in withholding his third son from Tamar) as well as the true identity of his consort, repents and forthrightly confesses his paternity.

Another set of twins enters the tradition and, again, supplanting takes place, but this time prenatally. Perez pushes Zerah aside, asserting the rights of the first born. As for Tamar and her act of liberation? She is not only the mother of Judah's children but also the ancestress of the Davidic dynasty. For a Canaanite who had a bad first marriage, her memory will always be associated with the royal purple of the kings of Israel.

~

Ephraim and Manasseh

Ephraim humbled himself, whereas Manasseh went out and assisted his father in his affairs. Therefore Ephraim was always placed before Manasseh.

(*Pesikta Rabbati* 3:93)

Someone said to Joseph, "Behold, your father is ill" (Gen. 48:1). Ephraim, who used to study Torah with Jacob, told Joseph of his father's illness.

(*Tanchuma, Vayechi* 6)

"An interpreter was between Pharaoh and Joseph" (Gen. 42:23). The interpreter was Manasseh.

(*Bereishit Rabbah* 91:8)

~

$\mathcal{W}$e're becoming accustomed to the pattern. The younger supercedes the older. Isaac has the last laugh in the rivalry with Ishmael. Jacob supplants Esau. Perez beats out Zerah by a "thread."[1] And Ephraim receives grandfather Jacob's blessing

---

1. In Gen. 38:27–30 Tamar gives birth to twins. The midwife tied a crimson thread to the hand of the child who first emerged from the womb. However, when the firstborn withdrew his hand, his brother emerged. This child was called Perez, meaning "breach." The child with the crimson thread on his hand was called Zerah, meaning "brightness."

before his elder brother Manasseh. It is the most famous invocation in Jewish history as Jacob, maneuvering his right hand upon the head of Ephraim (despite Joseph's protests), avers, "Manasseh also shall become a people, and he also shall be great; howbeit his younger brother shall be greater than he, and his seed shall become a multitude of nations" (Gen. 48:19). Then, turning to his grandchildren, he utters the blessing that would be invoked upon every generation of Jewish sons Sabbath eve: "God make thee as Ephraim and as Manasseh" (Gen. 48:20). By extension, Jewish daughters are blessed: "God make thee as Sarah, Rebecca, Rachel, and Leah."

By this time the reader is not surprised, particularly at the rabbinical liberties taken with the text. Because certain sentences in the Joseph story lack nominal references, the rabbis substitute, with ulterior motives, Manasseh and Ephraim. Thus the rabbis explain that Ephraim is the son who reports to his father of Jacob's illness. Like his grandfather, Ephraim stays close to home, "in the tent," and in the last seventeen years of his grandfather's life Ephraim has the blessed opportunity to study Torah with Jacob. Thus there is the closeness of heart and spirit between the two.

Manasseh has a different inclination. He follows the footsteps of his father, Joseph, not the path of Jacob. It is he whom the rabbis perceive as the intermediary when Joseph finally encounters his brothers in Pharaoh's court. It is an important role, yet it reveals the political nature of Manasseh, who is rewarded for his faithfulness, but on a less exalted level than the studious Ephraim. Perhaps Manasseh is Joseph's favorite—his father does try to rearrange Jacob's hands during the blessing, but finally Joseph does give in to Israel's wishes. He may be the viceroy of Egypt, but he would never disrespect his father.

Filial love, respect, honor, and Torah study were the traits that earned father's blessings. Although some wicked kings would be included among their descendants (Jeroboam, Ahab, Jehu), Jacob knew that Ephraim and Manasseh came from a marriage of holiness and were worthy of his benediction. All of us frail mortals pray for the same understanding.

Asenath

After the incident at Shechem, Jacob wrote on a gold foil all that had befallen with Hamor, father of Shechem. When Dinah gave birth to Asenath, he placed the foil about the infant's neck and cast her into the wall of Egypt. That day Potiphar went out to stroll with his servants. When they reached the "wall," they heard the sound of a baby crying. They took the child, and after Potiphar read Joseph's account he said: "This is the daughter of a great man. Take her to my house."

(*Midrash Aggadah, Bereishit* 41:45)

After Potiphar's wife falsely accused Joseph of attacking her, Potiphar sought to kill him until his daughter Asenath came secretly and defended Joseph's actions. The Holy One, Blessed is He, said: "Since you have spoken on Joseph's behalf, the tribes which I will raise from him will come through you."

(*Yalkut Shimoni, Vayeishev* 146)

*T*he career of Asenath, whose biblical parents are Potiphar and his mysteriously seductive yet unnamed wife, is befuddled by our rabbinical commentators who want to deliver the unfortunate Dinah from her ignominy. Dinah was the daughter of Leah and

Jacob, and her abduction and violation by Shechem brought about all forms of redress. The physical violation was reciprocated by Jacob's sons' brutal retaliation against Shechem's uncircumcised males. The psychological damage was repaired through the midrashic creation of Asenath's birth—an unwanted child from a damaged daughter of a patriarch who found her way back to her people in the most circuitous fashion.

Indeed, the story of Asenath is astonishing in both its literal and midrashic readings. Is she real or chimerical? The fantasy of Asenath, whose mother tried to tantalize the young Joseph, was realized in her eventual union with Joseph, the daughter winning out over the mother. The rabbis attempt to legitimize the mother–daughter struggle through attention to Asenath's sense of righteousness, but they fall a little short of depicting the true Freudian implications of this complex narrative.

Better to look to modern sources for this answer. In *Master of Dreams: The Jew in a Gentile World*,[1] the literary critic, Leslie-Fiedler explains: Joseph dreamed a dream of his greatness. Narcissistically, he wished to "make it" as a Jew in the gentile world. Asenath, the removed and forbidden woman, was part of the enticing package that awaited after he had rescued Egypt from famine. Joseph's dream couldn't have been greater. Everything he laid his eyes upon was his. For Asenath, whatever her origin— Egyptian or from Shechem—it was an unanticipated destiny of glory. Unquestionably, Asenath agreed to raise her children, Manasseh and Ephraim, as Jews. Like Ruth, Asenath knew what was best for everyone, but most of all, herself. Who knows what seed had been planted in Joseph's escapade with her mother?

---

1. Originally published in *Partisan Review*, Summer, 1967.

Miriam

Three good leaders arose for Israel: Moses, Aaron, and Miriam.

(*Taanit* 9a)

Who are the seven prophetesses? Sarah, Miriam, Deborah, Hannah, Abigail, Huldah, and Esther.

(*Megillah* 14a)

Why did Miriam stand from afar to see what would become of her baby brother Moses? Because she prophesied: "My mother is destined to bear a son who will redeem Israel."

(*Shemot Rabbah* 1:22)

One book closes; another opens. At the end of Genesis the descendants of Jacob and Joseph are well ensconced in Egypt. Unfortunately, their secure tenure is a mirage. A new Pharaoh comes to the throne and the Hebrews are both enslaved and persecuted. Indeed, all of Egypt has already been tyrannized because where a king is god all men are slaves.

Enter Miriam, Moses's sister who, not unlike Elizabeth of the New Testament (the mother of John the Baptist, who heralded the birth of the Christian savior), has prescience of Moses's greatness. When her mother, Jochebed, puts Moses into an ark of bulrushes and places it in the Nile, Miriam pursues the tiny vessel. After seeing it taken ashore by Pharaoh's daughter, she convinces the royal heiress to employ Jochebed, the mother, as a nursemaid.

Thus the pathway to Israel's future is paved. Although Moses is in Pharaoh's house and reared as an Egyptian prince, his pabulum is Jewish. More significantly, his sister continues to watch over and inspire him and the Israelites. Miriam stands at the head of the fledgling nation; after the drowning of the Egyptian army in the Red Sea, she leads the women in song, earning the title "prophetess" (Exod. 15:20–21).

According to the midrash, Miriam gives birth to Bezalel, the brilliant architect of Israel's desert tabernacle. From Bezalel comes the house of David. This is in addition to her gift of prophecy and wisdom. But she is sometimes too outspoken. In Numbers 12 she and Aaron speak against Moses because he had injudiciously married a Cushite woman. For this sin of calumny the Lord covers Miriam with leprosy. Moses pleads for the Lord to show mercy and Miriam is forgiven. Clearly his love and loyalty to her override any of the jealousy she displays toward him. Given the set of circumstances surrounding his birth, the full-grown baby brother, undeniably the Lord's greatest servant, has been not only charitable but correct in his forgiveness. She may have been called Miriam (in Hebrew *mar* means bitter) because at the time of her birth the Egyptians began to "embitter" the lives of the Israelites, but her sense of goodness, her prophetic insight, and her redoubtable loyalty toward her brothers and her people place her at the very highest rung of Israel's greatest heroes. Miriam, the prophetess.

Shiphrah/Jochebed

Shiphrah is Jochebed; Puah is Miriam.

(*Sotah* 11b)

"They saved the male children alive" (Exod. 1:18). Shiphrah and Puah collected water and food from the houses of the rich women and gave it to the poor women, who thus sustained their children. In addition, they prayed before the Holy One, Blessed is He, that the babies be born unblemished.

(*Shemot Rabbah* 1:15)

"And He made of them houses" (Exod. 1:21). Pharaoh attempted to kill them, but the Holy One, Blessed is He, concealed them by covering them like two beams of a house.

(*Midrash HaGadol, Shemot* 1:21)

The rabbis were clever to confer the names of the Hebrew midwives, Shiphrah and Puah, upon Moses's mother and sister. By assisting mothers at the time of childbirth they heroically defied Pharaoh's decree to kill every Hebrew male infant. This enhanced their role as "deliverers" of the Israelites, particularly that of the mother of the Jewish world's most important person. If biblical names are heeded literally, Miriam is a more active protagonist, and her mother the passive nursemaid. But connecting Jochebed to the midwife Shiphrah activates her character. Suddenly she acquires courage, cunning, and faith in her ability to preserve the future of the Jewish people. Shiphrah practiced the rabbinical principle that "the saving of a single life is the equivalent of saving the entire world."

(Mishnah Sanhedrin 4:5)

Why is she called Shiphrah ("beautiful")? The rabbis, always quick to resort to linguistic wordplay, suggest that when Moses was born she cleansed or beautified him. Because of her heroism the people of Israel multiplied at her hand; her deeds were pleasant before God; and she appeased Pharaoh for her daughter's words, for Miriam had stuck her nose up at Pharaoh.

(Shemot Rabbah 1:13)

Why was she called Jochebed ("God's honor")? At last, we exhume a biblical reference. Exodus 6:20 asserts: "And Amram took him Jochebed his father's sister to wife, and she bore him Aaron and Moses." Jochebed's face had a semblance of the Divine radiance. Because Jochebed feared the Holy One, He honored her with the birth of Moses.

(Shemot Rabbah 1:16)

ॐ

*W*hatever name we employ, we learn the intent of the text. Moses had a noble lineage. Jochebed was a daughter of the original Levi. When she and Puah, God-fearing midwives, were rewarded with "houses," these were not buildings. Because of their devotion to the Jewish people, they were rewarded with grand dynasties. Jochebed/Shiphrah becomes the ancestress of the Kohanim, the "priests," and the Levites; Miriam/Puah becomes an ancestress of David (*Sotah* 11b). How noble was their calling!

Pharaoh

"Jochebed brought Moses to Pharaoh's daughter, and he became her son" (Exod. 2:10). Pharaoh hugged and kissed him, and Moses took off Pharaoh's crown and placed it on his own head.

(*Shemot Rabbah* 1:26)

Pharaoh was proud of his foolishness. Said the Holy One, Blessed is He, to Moses, "There is nothing to be done with this fool except to hit him with a stick." Therefore Moses came to him with a staff.

(*Midrash HaGadol, Shemot* 7:16)

The Lord spared Pharaoh at the Red Sea, and he went and ruled in Nineveh. When the Holy One sent Jonah to Nineveh to prophesy about it and to destroy it, Pharaoh heard and, immediately rising from his throne, rent his garments, and dressed in sackcloth and ashes.

(*Yalkut Shimoni, Shemot* 176)

ﮔ

*T*here are archetypal biblical heroes; there are archetypal biblical villains. No villain occupies a greater stage than the Pharaoh, whose regime was broken by the God of the Israelites piece by piece. Indeed, one of the most penetrating messages of the Bible— for there is no greater national drama in Jewish history than the

Exodus from Egypt—is the personal vendetta waged by the Almighty against the tyranny of this king who saw himself as a god and was perceived as one. Moses is most certainly God's agent and is supplied with supernatural powers for the task at hand, but the Lord conducts the battle for freedom, orchestrating the Israelite rebellion and escape from the land of slavery.

It was all part of Divinity's plan. The idea was to inflame and antagonize the fearsome Egyptian leader to the boiling point and then embarrass, humiliate, and ultimately destroy Pharaoh in front of his minions and prove his gods as helpless. The purpose was to inspire Moses and the Israelites with *Yirat Adonai*: "fear of the Lord." It seemed to work, at least until the sojourn in the wilderness when new temptations threatened the unity of the fledgling nation.

Thus the rabbis portray Pharaoh as a clown, impetuous by nature and easy to fool. The infant Moses wittingly usurps the tyrant's crown, and as an adult he proves superior to the Egyptian king. Time and again Pharaoh doesn't seem to understand the nature of Moses's power and belief. But all this is carefully planned, and the Egyptian king's final awakening to Moses's great source of strength is that much more devastating because of Pharaoh's prolonged state of ignorance. When he finally recognizes the awesome and terrible nature of the Israelite God after the splitting of the Red Sea and the drowning of his legions, he drowns himself (*Mechilta, Beshalach* 2:6). Another midrash suggests that he became the despot of Nineveh, undone by the preaching of the seafaring Jonah. It seems, in either case, a watery end.

ॐ

Jethro

He had six names: Jether, Jethro, Hobab, Reuel, Putiel, and Keni. He was called Jether because through him one "additional" portion was added to the Torah. When he did good deeds, an extra letter was added to Jether, making it Jethro.

(*Mechilta, Yitro* 1:1)

At the time that Moses told Jethro, "Give me your daughter Zipporah as a wife," Jethro said to him, "Agree that your first son will be dedicated to the discovery of God through investigation and that the later progeny will be dedicated to the Name of Heaven." Moses agreed. "Swear to me," said Jethro. Moses swore.

(*Mechilta, Yitro* 1:1)

When Jethro saw that the Holy One had destroyed Amalek in this world and the next, he regretted his idol worship and repented, saying, "I should follow only the God of Israel."

(*Shemot Rabbah* 27:6)

ॐ

What children escape their parents' admonition to carefully observe the parental attitudes of their future spouses? In the case of Moses, who had already been reared in two nationally and religiously divergent households (Egyptian and Jewish), that age-old imprimatur was made all the more difficult because Moses met his future father-in-law on the lam. No one could have prepared the young fugitive (Moses had fled from Egypt after killing an Egyptian taskmaster) for the personality of the "priest of Midian." Indeed, the different shades of Jethro's character would make *The Three Faces of Eve* look normal.

Jethro is a Kohen but not a Jewish priest. He is an idolator, a political leader, a philosopher, and a trusted counselor and adviser to his ambitious, Divinely inspired son-in-law. Jethro is judicious and pragmatic. He knows Moses is the true and fearless leader of the people, particularly when the future general of Israel rescues his seven daughters from marauding shepherds at the watering hole. They immediately recognize what each can give to one another. "Moses desired to dwell with Jethro; and he gave his daughter Zipporah to Moses" (Exod. 2:21). In addition, Midian serves as the backdrop for Moses's mission. While tending his father-in-law's flock, the future leader of the children of Abraham, Isaac, and Jacob experiences the theophany of the burning bush. It is in this place in this moment in history that Moses understands his role as God's agent in leading the Israelites out of Egypt.

Important chapters intervene as Moses returns to Egypt and vitiates the reign of Pharaoh. After the crossing of the Red Sea, Moses reunites with his family, who had earlier returned to Midian while he led the Israelites out of slavery. Jethro exclaims his approval of Moses's mission and declares his loyalty: "Now I know that the Lord is the greatest of all the gods" (Exod. 18:11). Moses wins over his father-in-law, although moments later Jethro advises his brilliantly educated, overzealous son-in-law that he's taken too much responsibility upon himself. Moses listens and appoints judges to help govern the people. Although rarely invoked as one of the principal characters in Israel's destiny, Jethro's influence upon the new nation was profound. He was, as much as Zipporah, Moses's helpmate.

ⳤ

Zipporah

Whoever saw her would acknowledge her beauty. She is called Zipporah, meaning "look" and "see" how beautiful! She is called "the Cushite" (Num. 12:1) because just as the Cushite woman is distinguished from other women by the color of her skin, so too was Zipporah distinguished from other women by her beauty.

(*Sifre, Beha'alotcha* 99)

When the elders were appointed, all of Israel lit candles and rejoiced for them. Miriam saw the candles burning and asked Zipporah, "What are these candles for?" Zipporah told her. "Fortunate are the wives who see their husbands rise to high position," said Miriam. "Woe is to them," said Zipporah, "for henceforth their husbands will separate from them."

(*Yalkut Shimoni, Beha'alotcha* 738)

Another matriarchal beauty, this time of Cushite origin, joins the ranks of Israel. Zipporah, Jethro's daughter, meets her beloved Moses at the archetypal well, this time in the land of Midian. The Exodus narrative does not belabor the romance. Jethro gives Zipporah to Moses, and she bears a son called Gershom. The name expresses Moses's anxiety that he was "a stranger in a strange land."

(Exod. 2:21–22)

ॐ

$\mathcal{W}$hat are the fates of wives of *Gedolei Hador* ("Great men of the generation")? The answer is clearly drawn in both the biblical text and midrashic literature. Moses was the great man of his generation. His destiny as God's emissary to the present and future generations of Jewish people was prefigured. Each act of his life was fraught with political and religious significance. His desert forays, military brilliance, and dramatic dash remind one of T. E. Lawrence. Given the nature of his task—the mission to bring forth a group of Jews and make them a Jewish people—Moses was too busy to devote himself to Zipporah. It is hard to believe that nearly two millennia ago, in the midrash, Moses's wife and sister engaged in a discussion about life's trade-offs.

Zipporah was essentially on her own. Moses left for Egypt without his family to engage in a struggle that would serve as the basis for all future Jewish existence. Procuring Israel's freedom, leading his people to Mount Sinai and through forty years in the wilderness, and presiding as judge, general, and president of Congregation Benei Israel occupied all his time, and then some. How did she deal with his absence? She carried forth in the manner of the matriarchs of the House of Israel. The Bible speaks of "her two sons" (Exod. 18:3) because Zipporah had educated Gershom and Eliezer without Moses (*Zohar* 2:69b).

Even when Moses was present, Zipporah's strength of character emerged. When Moses failed to circumcise Gershom, and the Lord prepared to smite him because of his sin of omission, Zipporah "took a flint, and cut off the foreskin of her son, and cast it at his [Moses's] feet" (Exod. 4:25). By touching the foreskin to Moses's feet, Zipporah hoped the merit of the circumcision would ward off the Angel of Death. It was an honorable and prophylactic act.

It was an extraordinary destiny—one that involved sacrifice in every facet of her existence. Although she expressed regret over losing her husband to the cause of the Jewish nation, she maintained her dignity. She never became haughty or arrogant because of her esteemed position. She continued to act as a Cushite (i.e., simply) in poverty and kingship (*Midrash HaGadol, Bamidbar* 12:1).

Aaron

When Moses spoke, Aaron would bend his ear to listen in awe, and Scripture considers it as if he heard directly from the Holy One, Blessed is He.

(*Mechilta, Bo* 3)

Aaron knew that the golden calf had come to Israel through him. He rose, tied a rope of iron about his waist, and circulated throughout the camps of Israel. To whoever did not know prayer he taught prayer; to whoever did not know *keriat Shema* ("Recitation of the *Shema*") he taught *keriat Shema*; to whoever was not fluent in the essence of Torah he taught the essence of Torah.

(*Yalkut Shimoni, Shemot* 391)

"Aaron held his peace" (Lev. 10:3). Silence is a sign of being comforted.

(*Avot d'Rabbi Natan* 14:6)

Aaron's death was as difficult before the Holy One as the breaking of the Tablets.

(*Vayikra Rabbah* 20:12)

*I*t's never easy for an older sibling to acknowledge the superiority of a younger. Aaron, younger than Miriam yet three years older than Moses, was no sluggard, but his role in the formation of the Israelite nation was always "supporting." Although little is recounted about Aaron's birth and rearing, it is known he remained in Egypt while Moses was in Midian. And, as Exodus 4:14 tells us, he was an eloquent speaker. His marriage to Elisheba, daughter of Amminadab, allied him with one of the most distinguished families of the tribe of Judah. His brother-in-law Nahshon was a chieftain of Judah and an ancestor of David, thus the linkage between the two great institutions of Israel: the House of David and the House of Aaron.

So Aaron had *yichus* (pedigree) through marriage and through his own achievements, which earned him the crown of the priesthood. He also had *tsuris* (trouble), particularly when Moses ascended Mount Sinai and left him alone to deal with a frightened and fragmented Israel. The incident of the golden calf could have been his downfall, yet Aaron's role is mitigated in both the biblical narrative and the midrash. Indeed, in rabbinical literature, Aaron's granting the Israelites their moment of apostasy is viewed as a heroic delaying tactic. Explicating the verse, "Tomorrow shall be a feast to the Lord" (Exod. 32:5), the rabbis assert that Aaron's words were intended to redirect the people's intentions, thus replacing "feast to the calf" with "feast to the Lord" (*Vayikra Rabbah* 10:3). Aaron sought peace, not conflict.

It is a life of struggle, conflict, and compromise. Aaron's sons, Nadab and Abihu, are consumed by their offering of "strange fire" (Lev. 10:1–2). But Aaron, who has dedicated his life to the service of the sanctuary, "held his peace." In reward for his silent and dignified acceptance of God's decree, he was honored by the following commandment: "Drink no wine nor strong drink, thou, nor thy sons with thee, when ye go into the tent of meeting, that ye die not" (Lev. 10:9).

Considering all the exploits of his life, the difficulties surmounted while forging a religious people, it was not surprising that the Holy One found it so painful to take this loyal servant from the midst of Israel. Aaron dies atop Mount Hor at the age of 123, having transferred the crown of priesthood to his son, Eleazar. The Aaronite line had been established.

Nadab and Abihu

Nadab and Abihu raised a disturbance between the congregation of Israel and the Holy One, Blessed is He.

(*Zohar* 3:38b)

Moses and Aaron were going their way, and Nadab and Abihu were walking behind them. Said Nadab to Abihu, "When will these two old men die, and you and I lead the generation?" The Holy One said to them: "Let us see who will bury whom."

(*Sanhedrin* 52a)

Aaron's sons died because of four things: entering the Holy of Holies, offering a sacrifice that they had not been commanded to offer, bringing an alien fire, and failing to consult each other.

(*Vayikra Rabbah* 20:8)

The deaths of Nadab and Abihu were recorded in a few places in the Torah to teach that there was sadness in the presence of God about them, for they were beloved by the Lord.

(*Bamidbar Rabbah* 2:23)

After the erection of the Tabernacle, Aaron and his sons, Nadab and Abihu, were consecrated as the *kohanim*, priests of Israel. The sacrificial service was entrusted into their hands by Moses. Unfortunately, amidst the ceremony of such awesome religious joy, Nadab and Abihu "each took [a] fire-pan, placed incense upon it, and brought before the Lord an alien fire that He had not commanded. A fire came forth from before the Lord and consumed them, and they died."

(Lev. 10:1–2)

It is a disturbing as well as confusing narrative, particularly as Moses calms his bereft brother with the Divine explanation: "Through them who are nearest me I will be sanctified, and before all the people I will be glorifed" (Lev. 10:3). The text tells us that Aaron "held his peace" but, more likely, he was dumbfounded. What brought about the deaths of these novitiates? The commentators offer numerous possibilities. Some take the passage literally: that is, Nadab and Abihu erred in bringing their own incense into the Holy of Holies. Some suggest that the two sons of Aaron, so moved by the splendiferous heavenly fire God had earlier bestowed upon the Israelite offerings, wished to reciprocate with a display of their own love of God. The offering of incense was their means of expressing this boundless devotion, but that was not according to script(ure).

The midrash, trying to shore up the bewildering text and the terrible harshness of the punishment, suggests that Nadab and Abihu were *letzim* ("scoffers") who resented the authority invested in their father by Moses. Thus there is the plotting and scheming to undermine the older generation. Whatever their motives, this was not a happy scene in Israel's history. The dutiful Aaron, who had earlier served as the people's *kapparah* ("expiatory sacrifice") during the building of the golden calf, now must humble himself again. It is a bitter pill and, with respect to the later fate of his other two sons, Eleazar and Ithamar, it becomes harder and harder to swallow.

Ithamar and Eleazar

Aaron had other sons who deserved to be burned like Nadab and Abihu as it is written, ". . . the sons of Aaron who were left" (Lev. 10:11), but the merit of their father protected them.

(*Yoma* 87a)

Moses ordained for Israel eight priestly watches: four comprised of descendants of Eleazar and four comprised of descendants of Ithamar.

(*Taanit* 27a)

What was the order of learning? Moses learned directly from God. Aaron entered and Moses taught him his lesson. Aaron's sons entered and Moses taught them. The sons went up. Eleazar seated himself to the right of Moses, Ithamar to the left of Aaron.

(*Eruvin* 54b)

*I*s it not one of the strange ironies of the universe that the smallest points of contention often evoke the most severe reactions? No story depicts this anomaly better than the tragedy of Aaron's sons, Nadab and Abihu, who are snuffed out by God for daring to offer an "alien fire" during the consecration of the Tabernacle. The midrash presents a rationale for the extremity of their punishment, but it is not satisfying, even if the bereaved Aaron "holds his peace." Now, what about the "sons who were left" (Lev. 10:11)? If the dispute over the offering by Nadab and Abihu seems like much ado about nothing, the textual explication of Eleazar and Ithamar's bungling of the "sin offering" seems even more trivial.

How did these two survive the wrath of an angry God? Seemingly, by luck of the draw. That is, the Lord had already unleashed his fury on the unsuspecting Nadab and Abihu. The newest transgression committed by Eleazar and Ithamar takes place immediately following the family tragedy. If Aaron's remaining sons had also been cauterized, no rabbinical explanation would have been forthcoming. But there is chastisement from Moses, who wonders aloud how these errant children could have disobeyed the rules regarding the burning and eating of the sin offering. Eleazar and Ithamar have no response. However, their father finally rises to their defense, taking the responsibility for their actions as part of his role as High Priest. Fortunately Moses, God's agent, relents.

Not a fortuitous beginning. Yet Eleazar serves as High Priest after his father's death. He helps Moses conduct the census of the people on the plains of Moab, and he aids Joshua in the division of the Holy Land. The priestly family of Zadok traces itself to Eleazar, who is regarded as the ancestor of sixteen of the twenty-four priestly houses. Ithamar, the youngest son of Aaron, succeeds Eleazar as the High Priest. He is responsible for the duties of the Levites in the wilderness and supervises the Gershonites and Merarites, who helped construct and maintain the Tent of Meeting. The house of Eli traces itself to him. There was honor at last for the marked sons of Aaron.

Bezalel

Bezalel [meaning "in the shadow of God"] was so named for his wisdom.

(Berachot 55a)

Bezalel went up to Mount Sinai, where he was shown the construction of the Tabernacle as if it were already made in Heaven.

(Midrash Shir HaShirim, ed. Buber 32)

For Bezalel's extreme dedication to the building of the Tabernacle, the Holy One, Blessed is He, did not withhold his reward. Scripture made him known over every item that was constructed; that is, "Bezalel made the table, Bezalel made the altar. . . ."

(Shemot Rabbah 50:3)

"Bezalel made the Ark" (Exod. 37:1). Why did the other wise men who made the Tabernacle not make the Ark? Because Bezalel kept the covenant, he earned this privilege.

(Zohar 2:214b)

Bezalel knew how to join together the letters with which heaven and earth were created.

(Berachot 55a)

His destiny was revealed by the Holy One to Moses:

See, I have called by name Bezalel the son of Uri, the son of Hur, of the tribe of Judah; and I have filled him with the spirit of God, in wisdom,

and in understanding, and in knowledge, and in all manner of workmanship, to devise skillful works, to work in gold, and in silver, and in brass,
and in cutting of stones for setting, and in carving of wood, to work in all
manner of workmanship.

(Exod. 31:1–5)

ﺩﺝ

Not a bad curriculum vitae. Not only was he Divinely recom-
mended, Bezalel finished the work on time—that is, with
Oholiab's assistance. This master craftsman constructed the Tent
of Meeting, the Ark of the Testimony, the ark cover, the table
and its vessels, the candlestick, the altar and its vessels, and the
priestly garments for Aaron and his sons.

So redoubtable were Bezalel's skill and knowledge that the
Judeo-Greek philosopher, Philo, viewed the artisan as a symbol
of pure knowledge. Indeed, his very name begs for interpretation,
and the rabbis do not hesitate. Although his lineage is traced to
the aristocratic tribe of Dan, he transcends his earthly roots and
acquires an existence and a reputation that can only be described
as heavenly. Dwell "in the shadow of God" and great mysteries
shall be revealed to you. The meaning of Bezalel's name heralded
his future as an artist and artisan, though he could not possibly
have apprenticed for this craft in the wilderness.

Whence his greatness? Whence the greatness of any of
Judaism's *Gedolei Hador* ("exalted of the Generation")? Bezalel's
story adheres to a common biblical motif: it was all preordained.
Bezalel was "called by name" (Exod. 31:1) to understand the secret of the Tabernacle and its vessels.

Loved and adored by his admiring contemporaries and awe-
struck future religionists, Bezalel was granted five other names:
Reaiah ("the seer"), Shobal ("the builder of the dovecote"—a syn-
onym for the Tabernacle), Jahat ("the dreadful"), Ahumai ("the
unifier of Israel"), and Lahad ("one who beautified Israel" or "one
who was near to the poor") (*Shemot Rabbah* 40:4).

Korah

The members of Korah's company have no share in the World to Come because of their dispute with Moses and Aaron.

(*Sanhedrin* 109b)

The Levite with the greatest potential was Korah, whom the Holy One created on earth in the image of the heavenly. He was named Korah ("bald") at the time he was shaven.

(*Zohar* 3:49a)

Korah was a great scholar, one of the bearers of the ark.

(*Bamidbar Rabbah* 18:3)

Our teacher Moses asked the Holy One, Blessed is He, to deal with Korah not through the attribute of mercy, but through the attribute of strict justice.

(*Mishnat Rabbi Eliezer* 5)

He was born a Levite which, as we have seen with respect to the destinies of Aaron's children (who died fulfilling their role as Temple servants), put him on shaky ground. Indeed, in Korah's case this was literally true: "The earth opened its mouth and swallowed all the people who were with Korah, and all their goods."

(Num. 16:32)

*T*he wilderness period, under the guidance of Moses, was a group effort. There was little room for individual expression. Divinity was in no mood to be challenged, and when He was provoked, both heaven and earth were deployed to administer the punishment. And yet, this tragedy involved much more than God's concern regarding improper sacrificial offerings. Korah was angry that Aaron and his sons had been elevated to the high priesthood. Thus, typifying a rebel leader, he posed as a champion of the people, trying to discredit the leadership of Moses and Aaron. Directly confronting his adversaries he declaims, "It is too much for you! For the entire assembly—all of them—are holy and the Lord is among them; why do you exalt yourselves over the Lord's congregation" (Num. 16:3)?

After this challenge, in the manner of the Wild West, the two factions select their weapons. Firepans are placed before the altar. The Lord will decide which offering is acceptable. The outcome? It is so obvious the rabbis wonder why Korah, a respected Levite and scholar, had acted so brazenly. They surmise that Korah, blinded by ambition, saw prophetically that the prophet Samuel would be among his offspring, which would include twenty-four groups of Levites (*Bamidbar Rabbah* 18:2). This vision encouraged him to believe that he would not die in the revolt. Unfortunately for Korah, this was a tragic miscalculation. His sons would repent and survive, while he and his 250 upstarts were swallowed by the earth. According to the Talmud, the place in which the rebels were buried still has smoke arising from it. If one draws near, he hears voices saying, "Moses and his Torah are true, and we are liars" (*Sanhedrin* 110a).

Witnessing this desert phenomenon, one questions why any of the Israelites had the courage to speak with Moses, let alone the chutzpah to challenge his authority.

_ೲ_

Balaam

There never arose philosophers the likes of Balaam son of Beor.
(*Eichah Rabbah Pesikta* 2)

An evil eye, a haughty spirit, and a lusting soul are signs of the disciples of the wicked Balaam.
(*Pirkei Avot* 5:22)

Balaam was granted prophecy for the benefit of Israel.
(*Vayikra Rabbah* 1:12)

"Those who bless you are blessed, and those who curse you are cursed" (Num. 24:9). Since Balaam was an enemy, he began with a blessing and ended with a curse, for the ending is more significant than the beginning.
(*Bereshit Rabbah* 66:4)

_ೲ_

*T*here are few more curious biblical tableaus than the description of Balaam riding a reluctant donkey in the plains of Moab in order to curse the advancing nation of Israel. Curious and hilarious, as the donkey not only disobeys Balaam's command to "stay the course" but seems to perceive, more than this cunningly brilliant and deceptive prophet, God's miraculous handiwork. Balaam is even orally reprimanded by this beast of burden, who retorts to Balaam's threats, "Am I not your she-donkey that you have ridden all your life until this day?" (Num. 22:30). Does her lifelong service to her master mean anything at all to him?

What the donkey had seen was none other than the angel of the Lord blocking the passageway with a drawn sword. Balaam's eyes were closed to this phenomenon, but eventually he was enlightened. It is all part of God's plan, an angry Divinity, who is furious that Balaam has agreed to carry out the Moabite King Balak's plan to curse the Israelites. Although portrayed as a fool and forever identified with the talking donkey, Balaam was perceived rabbinically as the last of the prophets of the nations and as one who surpassed Moses in the wisdom of sorcery (*Tanna d'Bei Eliyahu Rabbah* 28).

Not unlike the episode of the Pharaoh, the more belligerent Balaam becomes, the greater the demonstration of God's might and the evil prophet's weakness. He becomes a tool of the Almighty, reversing the curses of Balak into Israel's most glorious blessings. Like the most humble penitent, the prophet utters blessings that are so praiseworthy the sages fixed them permanently in the daily liturgy. The Lord wanted these sublime utterances to come to Israel through the agency of the wicked and immoral Balaam, so that all the world would know that everyone was helpless to harm Israel against God's will. Despite himself, Balaam becomes God's vessel of religious steadfastness, as he declaims, "How goodly are your tents, O Jacob" (Num. 24:5). The rabbis understand this sentence as a reference to Israel's synagogues and houses of study. Sent to presage victory for the arrogant King of Moab, Balaam ends his prophetic career with a paean to the greatest glory of our people, our liturgical and intellectual inheritance.

꙳

Phineas

One should always cleave to people of good character, as we see from Aaron, who married Amminadab's daughter and had Phineas as his grandson.

(Bava Batra 109b)

Phineas did not become a priest until he had slain Zimri. Rav Ashi says: until he made peace among the tribes of Reuben, Gad, Manasseh, and Israel.

(Zevachim 101b)

Not for naught did Phineas go to war against the Midianites, but to exact retribution for his ancestor Joseph, of whom it is written: "The Midianites had sold him to Egypt."

(Gen. 37:36) *(Sotah* 43a)

꙳

*T*he narrative of Phineas, son of Eleazar, grandson of Aaron, surrounds the account of Balaam, Israel's "anti-Prophet." It is more than a literary encirclement. The beleaguered Balaam is finally slain by the zealous priest of Israel in Numbers 31. But Phineas is more recognized for his first act of "speardom" as he pierces an Israelite man and Midianite woman engaging in harlotry directly in front of the Tent of Assembly (Num. 25:8). This immorality had been encouraged by Balaam who, frustrated by his inability to curse the people of Israel, employs the Moabites and Midianites to entice Jewish men to debauchery. Until Phineas's moral thrust the plot had been successful.

It was so successful that the "wrath of the Lord flared up against Israel" (Num. 25:3). Twenty-four thousand Israelites died in a plague in retribution for the orgy of immorality with forbidden women. But Phineas's heroism ended the devastation. His reward? First, an entire chapter of the Torah is named eponymously for him. Second, the Lord tells Moses, "Behold! I give him My covenant of peace. And it shall be for him and his offspring after him a covenant of eternal priesthood, because he took vengeance for his God, and he atoned for the Children of Israel" (Num. 25:12–13).

Phineas now ascends from the level of Levite to Kohen, and his descendants will be High Priests—from warrior to religious leader. But as indicated above, he also returned to battle against the Midianites (who quite coincidentally had sold his ancestor, Joseph, into bondage). The Midianites were summarily punished because of their responsibility for the Jewish sins of immorality and idolatry. Phineas is included in this military incursion because God wanted the entire nation to know that Phineas had rescued them from utter calamity and was thereby deserving of eternal reward.

Millennia later, Phineas became the memorable character of John Knowles's tome, *A Separate Peace*. The biblical character was a fighter for God's righteousness; the hero of Knowles's book was a wonderful, lilting, pacific, lamb-like figure. Both ultimately achieved peace, but in remarkably different ways.

Amalek

What reason had Amalek to settle on the border on the way of the Israelites' entry into the Land? His grandfather Esau had commanded him to encounter them on the way, so he uprooted himself and resettled there.

(*Bamidbar Rabbah* 16:18)

The Holy One, Blessed is He, took an oath by His throne of glory not to leave a single descendant of Amalek under heaven so that it should not be said, "This tree was Amalek's, this camel was Amalek's, this lamb was Amalek's. . . ." Neither the name nor the throne is complete until the memory of Amalek is eradicated.

(*Shocher Tov* 9:10)

*S*ome personalities take root in our consciousness because of their heroic deeds and inherent goodness; others become internalized as paradigms of evil. Amalek and his "kind" are indelibly fixed in the Jewish text as the earliest representatives of a bitter and virulent form of anti-Semitism. Tracing their ancestry to Esau was no cause for rejoicing. These were Israel's incessant foes, constantly seeking to attack the rearguard of our people.

First encountered in Exodus 17:8–16, the Amalekites attacked the Israelites after the crossing of the Red Sea. Joshua fought off the enemy's thrusts while Moses, viewing the battle from a distance, was literally supported by Aaron and Hur. By literally helping the Israelite leader lift his arms to God, Aaron and Hur enabled Moses to symbolically lift the Israelites to victory. Amalek escaped to confront our people time and again throughout the pages of the Bible. At the end of the war Moses was commanded to write that the Lord would one day blot out the memory of Amalek from under the heaven. He actually built an altar of victory (à la Greeks) that he called *Adonai-Nissi*, "the Lord is my miracle," as a reminder of the perpetual war that was to be waged against the evil adversary.

And war is continually waged against Amalek, with concomitant success and failure. The Amalekites pursued the Israelites through the period of the Judges and participated in the capture of Jericho (Judg. 3:12–13). The decisive clash, however, was postponed to the era of the monarchy. Saul was commanded to smite Amalek and destroy his people, "infant and suckling, ox and sheep, camel and ass" (1 Sam. 15:3). Unfortunately, Saul does not complete the task, a sin that costs him the support of the Lord and His prophet Samuel.

From the first attack upon the Israelites at Rephidim Amalek becomes Israel's mortal adversary. In addition, he becomes the prototype of evil in each generation. The wicked Haman is his descendant. Further, he is concretized in a Deuteronomic passage to "remember what Amalek did to you when you left Egypt . . . and when you possess the Land of Israel you shall wipe out the memory of Amalek from under the heaven—you shall not forget" (Deut. 25:17–19). It is a positive commandment to erase the memory of Amalek as well as to remember his evil, cowardly deeds in order to inspire hatred of him. It is a splendid literary contradiction, as we are ultimately enjoined to remember Amalek's treachery orally and never to remove his inimical memory from our hearts.

Joshua

The face of Moses was like the sun, the face of Joshua like the moon.

(Bava Batra 75a)

Although Scripture calls Joshua *Hosea*, it is not to disparage him. Rather, it is to indicate that he was Hosea before he was promoted to high position, and he was Hosea thereafter (he remained as humble and righteous as before).

(Tosefta Berachot 1:16)

"The servant of Moses" (Num. 11:28). It is an honor for Joshua to be known in this manner. From the case of Joshua our Sages derive the principle: "Serving Torah scholars is greater than learning the Torah."

(Lekach Tov, Bamidbar 11:28)

Moses received the Torah from Sinai and transmitted it to Joshua; and Joshua to the elders. . . .

(Pirkei Avot 1:1)

"He shall cause them to inherit the Land" (Deut. 3:28). This teaches that Joshua was not to depart this world until he had given Israel possession of the Land.

(Sifre Pinchas 136)

"His firstling, majesty is his" (Deut. 33:17). This refers to Joshua, who caused the sun and the moon to stand still. When the Holy One appeared to Joshua,

He found him sitting with the Book of Deuteronomy in his hand. The Lord said to him, "Strengthen yourself, Joshua, persevere, Joshua. . . ." Joshua took the Book, displayed it before the sun, and said, "Because I have not ceased from studying this Book, you must cease from moving at my request." Immediately, "the sun's movement ceased, and the moon stood still."

(Josh. 10:13) (*Bereishit Rabbah* 6:9)

*I*n a world obsessed with nomenclature, the word "servant" is a pejorative. Yet in the pages of the Bible a servant (*mesharet*) had considerable standing in the community. How much more so the *mesharet Moshe* (Moses)? Yes, Joshua, nee Hosea, served the greatest of all the biblical personalities, and he did so with a fierceness of devotion and loyalty that made a deep and lasting impression upon Moses, his teacher.

Joshua was aware of his subordinate role, but rather than be diminished by it, he cherished and honored his place in the Israelite hierarchy, thus earning not only his master's blessing but the blessing of the Master of the Universe. Called upon to fight with Amalek, "Joshua weakened Israel's hated adversary with the blade of the sword" (Exod. 17:13). During this battle Moses stayed behind, watching his young disciple lead Israel to victory. Moses's act indicated the type of leader he was. He knew Joshua's destiny was to bring the people into the Land; therefore, he sought to train him in warfare by pushing him forward, all the while observing in the background.

Joshua exhibited the confidence Moses displayed in him during the mission of the spies. Supported by Caleb, he contradicted the majority report of the other ten tribes, who expressed fear at the dangers that would befall them in the Promised Land. Together the faithful pair exclaimed, "The land, which we passed through to spy it out, is an exceeding good land" (Num. 14:7). This was the answer the Lord had expected. The optimistic Caleb and Joshua would enter the Land; the pessimists would not. All would endure a forty-year punishment in the wilderness.

Because of his military, intellectual, and spiritual acumen Joshua was rewarded with the task of leading the Israelites into the Promised Land. His role would dramatically change from that of faithful servant to Israelite general because in his Pentateuchal career, his contributions, though manifold, were in the service of God and Moses. Indeed, according to tradition, Joshua faithfully wrote down the last eight verses of the Torah, the narrative of his master's death (*Bava Batra* 14b).[1]

As the Book of Deuteronomy closes, Joshua takes up the reins of leadership, blessed by his patron Moses, and "full of the spirit of wisdom" (Deut. 34:9). It was, after all the sojourns and wilderness crises, all the attendant fears and anxieties, a comparatively quick and successful campaign to conquer the Promised Land. Or was it? The question is a natural one, and not only on account of the Israelites' difficulty throughout the wilderness period. There were many adversaries in Canaan; further, the Book of Judges has led many scholars to surmise that the original conquest of the Land presented by Joshua was neither as comprehensive nor decisive as it is represented here.

What is represented here is a theology and a succession of leadership from one generation to the next. Joshua is entrusted with the generalship of a new nation and is advised by his Commander-in-Chief: "Only be strong and very courageous, being careful to do according to all the law which Moses my servant commanded you . . . for the Lord your God is with you wherever you go" (Deut. 1:9). Judging the contents of Joshua's book alone, we see that the Lord's declaration is supported not only by Joshua's military successes but by the miracles and signs with which he is also empowered.

His entire life was one of devotion, one of service, one of loyalty. The adding of the letter *yod* to his name, a letter that had been taken from Sarah's original name Sarai, was the symbolic representation of the increased honor and reverence later bestowed upon the humble leader. The *mesharet Moshe*, Moses's servant, was now the *eved Adonai*, the Lord's servant. Joshua/Hosea, our great leader, our great follower, the successor of Moses, the leader of the conquest of Canaan.

---

1. Another opinion asserts that God dictated the final eight verses of the Torah to Moses, and he wrote them with tears rather than ink (*Bava Batra* 15a).

Moses

The greatest prophet of Israel, *Moshe Rabbeinu* (Moses our Rabbi), imparts through his death a distinct lesson: all of us, great and small, are given the breath of life by our Creator. When the Creator decrees it, our lives, no matter how great or small, once again belong to Him.

GREATNESS

Moses was equal to Israel, and Israel to Moses (*Mechilta Yitro* 1:1). From the day Moses was born, the Divine Presence never departed from him (*Zohar* 1:120b).

PROPHET

Our teacher Moses gazed through a clear glass. [That is, his prophetic vision was clear] (*Yevamot* 49b).

None of the prophets knew precisely what they were prophesying, except for Moses and Isaiah (*Shocher Tov* 90:4).

HUMILITY ,

"The man Moses was exceedingly humble" (Num. 12:3). He was a giant in humility (*Midrash HaGadol, Bamidbar* 12,3).

RADIANCE

From the sparks that emanated from the mouth of the Divine Presence when the Holy One taught him Torah, Moses had rays of glory (*Tanchuma, Ki Tisa*).

REDEMPTION

The Lord assessed all human beings but found no better messenger through whom to take Israel out of Egypt than our teacher Moses (*Pesikta Rabbati, Hosafah* 3).

SPLITTING OF THE RED SEA

Moses told the Israelites, "Come and cross the Red Sea." They said, "How can we pass between those walls of water?" He made it like a fertile valley. It sprouted greenery and the people pastured in it (*Shocher Tov* 114:7).

MOUNT SINAI

The first commandment went forth from the mouth of the Lord like sparks, lightning, and a flame. It flew through the air, appeared above the camp of Israel, then returned to be engraved on the

Tablets of the Covenant, which were in Moses's hand, where it penetrated from front to back. And so it was with each commandment (*Targum Yonatan, Shemot* 20:2).

ENDURING MERIT

The world exists only because of the merit of Moses and Aaron (*Chullin* 89a).

SHORTCOMINGS

Moses and Aaron died on account of their sins (*Shabbat* 55b).

DAY OF DEATH

The Holy One took away Moses's soul with a kiss of the mouth (*Devarim Rabbah* 11:8).

Deborah

Deborah dwelt in the city of Ataroth. She was independently wealthy. She owned palm trees in Jericho, orchards in Ramah, oil-producing olives in Beth-El, and white earth in Tur Malka.

(*Targum Shoftim* 4:5)

In the Song of Deborah, the women preceded the men, because here the redemption came through women: Deborah and Jael.

(*Lekach Tov, Shemot* 15:20)

If a prophet is haughty, his prophecy departs from him. We learn this from Deborah. After she boasted, "Until I arose, Deborah" (Judg. 5:7), her prophecy departed, and she cried, "Awake, awake, Deborah" (Judg. 5:12).

(*Pesachim* 66b)

꒜

*D*eborah, the wife of Lappidoth, was a prophetess and a judge of Israel. She sat under a palm tree hearing the cases of the Isra- elites. She had all the trappings of a good life: capital, career, and a healthy partnership. It was a marriage that had all the earmarks of modernity, although scholars date the period of Judges to the twelfth century B.C.E.

As Ayn Rand might ask, "Who was Deborah?" Not only is she unique as a woman prophetess and judge, but she is also seen as "a mother in Israel" (Judg. 5:7). Thus, she is an amalgam of Judaism's view of traditional motherhood (as rendered in Chapter 32 of Proverbs—"The Woman of Valor") and the independent woman who seemed, without biblical precedent, to invent herself along the way.

And what a way it was. When Israel is threatened by a Canaanite adversary, Deborah enlists the generalship of Barak, who "discomfits" Sisera and his legions. With the prescience of the difficulties to be faced by every generation of women seeking recognition for their accomplishments, she admonishes Barak before the campaign saying, "The journey that thou takest shall not be for thy honor; for the Lord will give Sisera over into the hand of a woman" (Judg. 4:9). This becomes a literal truth as Jael (prefiguring the slaying of Holofernes by Judith) slays Sisera, who mistakenly takes refuge in her tent.

Barak triumphs and joins his friend, the Judge, in an antiphonal song. Unfortunately, as seen through rabbinical lenses, Deborah sings of herself too boastingly. Because of this arrogant act she is deprived of the spirit of prophecy for a short period. Yet she gains the Lord's favor again and, like Hannah, one of Scripture's most sympathetic characters, she composes praises unto the Lord unsurpassed by all the writings of men. She received the secret of Divine wisdom and explicated her gift with exquisite grandeur.

Who was Deborah? Better perhaps to ask, "Who wrote the story of Deborah?" Most assuredly, this stunning narrative was written by a proto-Semitic-feminist.

Samson

The law courts of Gideon, Jephthah, and Samson are to be considered in their generations as equal to those of Moses, Aaron, and Samuel in their generations.

(Yerushalmi Rosh Hashanah 2:8)

Samson desired something impure (marriage to a heathen woman); therefore his life became dependent on something impure [the donkey's jawbone, which miraculously provided him with water].

(Rashi, Sotah 9b)

Five were created with one feature of supernatural perfection, and all were stricken in that feature. One was Samson in his strength: "His strength went from him" (Judg. 16:19).

(Sotah 10a)

"Remember me, I pray You, and strengthen me."

(Judg. 16:28)

Samson said before the Lord, "Remember to my credit that for twenty-two years I judged the people of Israel and never asked one of them to do so much as move a stick for me."

(Sotah 10a)

Samson was born because of his mother's beseechment of an angel of God. Prefiguring the birth and destiny of the prophet Samuel through the prayer of Hannah, Samson's unnamed mother accepts the heavenly decree to raise Samson as a Nazirite. The imperative is clear: "No razor shall come upon his head" (Judg. 13:5). Therein lies Samson's distinctiveness and his problem. When the angel left Manoah and his wife, it was in a flash of fire, foreshadowing Samson's illustriousness and his unbridled passion, which suffused his amorous and dangerous existence.

Was his name an accident? *Shemesh* means sun in Hebrew. The story, which is comprised of smaller stories (pericopae) has a decidedly literary bent. Samson pursues his enemy, the Philistines, with an unknown power of God's Divine purpose. He succeeds mightily. He pursues the Philistine women in the same manner but discovers, unwittingly, that they are as faithful to their nation as he is to Israel. This leads to infidelity, treachery, and Delilah and, eventually, to Hedy Lamarr and Victor Mature.

It *is* a story for a Hollywood agent. The beleaguered Samson gets no rest. If he is not serving Israel as judge, he is fighting Philistines with the jawbone of an ass, or he is posing unsolvable riddles to his consorts. Unfortunately, he cannot resist giving them the solutions. Unlike the answers to the *New York Times* crossword puzzle, these unwise revelations bring torture and death to Samson as well as to the Philistines, particularly his revelation to Delilah that shearing his uncut Nazirite hair would rob him of his godly strength.

Captured, weakened, his eyes put out, mocked, and chained between two pillars in a great Philistine palace, he prefigures a martyr from the New Testament, except this judge of the Jewish people does not die passively. Summoning all his remaining strength, he brings down the house, smiting his hated adversaries whom he had alternately hated and loved throughout his volatile and ambivalent life.

Hannah

On Rosh Hashanah, Sarah, Rachel, and Hannah were granted conception.

(Berachot 29a)

There were two women who uttered songs and praises to the Holy One, Blessed is He, such as no man in the world ever uttered. Who were they? Deborah and Hannah.

(Zohar 3:19b)

"Hannah prayed" (1 Sam. 2:1) with prophetic inspiration. She said, "My son Samuel is destined to be a prophet in Israel, and in his days Israel will be miraculously saved from the Philistines.

(Targum Shmuel 1:2:1)

*P*rayer and conception, at least in the biblical world, went together like milk and honey. Maternity in the Bible, except for Sarah's conceiving of Isaac, was no laughing matter. There were tears of loyalty to patriarchs that allowed surrogate births, and there was righteous anger directed toward those surrogates when they threatened to usurp the matriarchs' family seats. (See the discussion of Hagar.)

None of this should surprise, especially when one considers the role of parenthood and inheritance prescribed in Scripture.

In a fantastic sense, this struggle was often sensed within the mother's womb, as attested to in the births of Jacob and Esau, and Perez and Zerah. Primogeniture meant everything; then again, famous grandfathers made famous decisions about which grandson should receive the principal blessing. Sometimes famous matriarchs helped alter the course of family (then tribal) history.

In the case of Hannah, however, there was no subterfuge, just pathos. Married to Elkanah, an Ephraimite, she watched forlornly over the particular fecundity of the second spouse Peninnah. Elkanah sought to reassure Hannah of her preciousness by giving her twice the sustenance of her marital rival. Unfortunately, Hannah was growing fat but not happy. Hannah wept before Elkanah and, despite his comforting words, remained inconsolable.

But this was a resourceful matriarch. Having already endured a life without childbirth, she was prepared to endure another loss in exchange for the gift of a prophet in Israel. Praying silently for a son unto the "Lord of Hosts" (1 Sam. 1:11), the first time the God of Israel is called by this name, she promises the "manchild" will serve his people and the priesthood. Eli, the priest, is suspicious of Hannah's meditations, even questioning her sobriety, but Hannah convinces him of her sorrowful condition and her sincerity. More than that, Eli is the recipient of the promise Hannah was to uphold. After her prayers are answered and Samuel is born and weaned, Hannah brings the precocious lad to the stodgy uncomprehending priest, who has to be convinced of the child's gifts of prophecy.

Hannah's beseeching of God was cited by the Sages as a model of prayer. She prayed with devotion, moved her lips to pronounce the words, and prayed from her heart in a soft voice (*Berachot* 31a-b). Hannah, the most "gracious" mother of our people.

Samuel

Hannah prayed, "Give to your handmaid a manchild" (1 Sam. 1:11); that is, a man distinguished among men. Samuel said: "A son who will anoint two men, Saul and David." Rabbi Yochanan said: "A son who is equivalent to two men, Moses and Aaron."

(*Berachot* 31b)

When the people of Israel saw the cloud suspended between heaven and earth, they knew that God was speaking with Moses. So it was also with Samuel.

(*Sifrei Zuta, Bamidbar* 12:5)

Samuel wrote the book of Samuel, and in addition Judges and Ruth. The book of Samuel was completed by Gad the Seer and Nathan the prophet.

(*Bava Batra* 14b, 15a)

The righteous Samuel went throughout all the Israelite towns to judge the people.

(*Shabbat* 56a)

Samuel aged prematurely because of the trouble with his sons.

(*Aggadat Bereishit* 41)

*H*is mother had made a cosmic bargain: the gift of her son to Divine service in exchange for the greater glory of Israel. Thus Samuel's fate is prefigured, and his book is one of the most inventive and gripping narratives in the biblical corpus. He was a judge and a prophet, and later a counselor, adviser, and anointer of Israel's first kings.

Though he served the mighty and the Almighty, Samuel's task was not an easy one, as he watched Israel eventually reject a theocracy, succumbing to the secular rule of a king. This inspired the most antipolitical invective in the Bible, as Samuel, excoriating his people, forewarns of the "manner of the king that shall reign over them" (1 Sam. 8:9). The Israelites learn that their sons will be conscripted, their daughters pressed into culinary service, their fields confiscated, their lands taxed, their cattle tithed, and they themselves enslaved. *Gornicht helfen.* Having heard Samuel's premonitions, they insist on receiving a king so that "we also may be like all the nations" (1 Sam. 8:20).

Samuel wasn't one to say "I told you so," but subsequent events fulfill his dire prophecy. The political intrigue of a nascent monarchy challenges the absolute religion of the righteous judge. He witnesses the rise and fall of the beleaguered Saul and that leader's desperate and shameful treatment of his successor, Israel's greatest prodigy, David. Samuel holds his own during these stressful times, but the years take their toll. His sons, the judges of the next generation, prove far more corruptible than the redoubtable prophet, and he ages prematurely. Yet he is called upon one more time for counsel—from his grave!—by an even more desperate King Saul looking for his mentor's blessing. With no political obligations remaining in the afterlife, the weary counselor of kings tells the harsh truth: because Saul did not fully execute the Lord's instructions to eradicate Amalek, the Philistines will conquer Israel. Samuel's words are upheld. Honest to the end, and even beyond.

◈

Saul

O, beware, my lord, of jealousy!
It is the green ey'd monster which doth mock
The meat it feeds on.
(Othello, 3.3.165)

"There was no man among the Children of Israel better than he" (1 Sam. 9:2). In every respect? Therefore, it is written, "From his shoulders and upward he was better than any of the people" (1 Sam. 9:2)—that is, only in that respect.
(Yerushalmi, Sotah 1:8)

"Behold, he has hidden among the baggage."
(1 Sam. 10:23)

When they came to anoint him, he said, "Go ask the Urim veTumim (priestly oracles) whether I am worthy, and if I am not, leave me in my place."
(Midrash Aggadah, Vayikra 1:1)

Saul was equivalent to all David's enemies put together.
(Shocher Tov 7:13)

◈

*T*he tragedy of King Saul, reminiscent of Shakespeare's studies of Richard the Third and Othello, is adumbrated in Samuel's "young and goodly" son of Kish, who hails from the humble tribe of Benjamin, must rise and fall, so predictive are the prophet's warnings.

The tragedy becomes more devastating when one considers Saul's earliest inclinations. His grand stature was equalled only by his humility. Faced with Israel's first secular mission, Saul "hides among the baggage" (1 Sam. 10:23), whence the reluctant king is fetched and installed in office. "Reluctant" is the salient adjective in the narrative. "Ambivalent" is another that must be added to Saul's emotional composition. That ambivalence manifests itself with the rise of the brilliant warrior, poet, and statesman, David. Saul admires, loves, reveres, and then disdains, hates, and undermines the future king of Israel. The concoction is further embittered by his son Jonathan's love for the erstwhile shepherd. Thrown in for good measure is Saul's daughter Michal, who is given to David as a wife in order to make him more susceptible to the attacks of the Philistines.

Nothing could prevent David's meteoric rise, nor his immense popularity with the people of Israel and Judah. Saul's anger turns into incoherent rage as he tries, literally, to pierce the mysterious veil that protected the son of Jesse. By the end of the first book of Samuel, the raving, maniacal Saul is reduced to a proto-Semitic version of Macbeth, conjuring up the ghost of his trusted adviser Samuel who, awakened from his eternal rest, lets the doomed king know he never approved of him in the first place. Confronting his Philistine adversaries, Saul falls finally on his sword and dies a victim of his numerous internal demons, without a kingdom and minus a horse.

Jonathan

An example of love that did not depend on a specific cause is the love of David and Jonathan.

(Pirkei Avot 5:19)

Three abandoned their crowns in This World and inherited the life of the World to Come. One of them was Jonathan, son of Saul.

(Yerushalmi, Pesachim 6:1)

". . . the soul of Jonathan was knit with the soul of David, and Jonathan loved him as his own soul."

(1 Sam. 18:1)

*T*he narrative of Jonathan, Saul's son, remains one of the more pathetic sections (in the Greek sense) in the Bible. He is a young man, who within his brief and tragic life, evinces gifts of generalship and profound sensitivity. Jonathan confronts his angry and jealous father, the King, in an attempt to prevent him from killing his beloved friend, David.

It is a complex weave. Handsome, poetic, irrepressible David is first embraced by Saul and Jonathan, but because of his unlimited success in war and his unrivaled popularity the young Bethlehemite soon incurs the wrath of the troubled King, whose raging pathologies subvert his genuine concern for his people.

Jonathan is placed in the middle, not only ducking the spears hurled in David's and his direction, but fielding the scorn and wrath directed toward himself as well. Acting courageously and living dangerously, Jonathan disobeys Saul's commandment: "Cursed be the man that eateth any food until it be evening, and I be avenged on mine enemies" (1 Sam. 14:24). Jonathan prefigures his destiny as his "eyes brighten from a taste of the forbidden honey."

This was a *vorspeise* of Jonathan's forbidden relationship with David, a love that was as precious as any in the history of literature, including that of the sentimental Queequeg and diffident Ishmael. That David and Jonathan loved each other was clear in every action Jonathan took to protect the "newborn king." All kinds of plots and schemes were hatched to preserve David's life, but the most fanciful is Jonathan's Cupidlike shooting of arrows to warn David of imminent danger from his father. Surely, the two-pronged weapons represent Jonathan's filial rebellion as well as his penetrating love for young David.

The arrows lead the way to David's escape and eventual ascension to the throne. Sadly, Jonathan is not able to ascend as well and is consigned to fight by his father's side in the futile battle against the Philistines on Mount Gilboa. Saul and his three sons die. The new king, discovering the fate of his beloved, mourns mightily:

> How are the mighty fallen in the midst of the battle!
> Jonathan upon thy high places is slain!
> I am distressed for thee, my brother Jonathan;
> Very pleasant hast thou been unto me;
> Wonderful was thy love to me,
> Passing the love of women.
>
> (2 *Sam*. 1:25–26)

꒰ꕤ꒱

Michal

Saul's children, Michal and Jonathan, both loved David. Michal helped him escape from inside the house, while Jonathan helped from outside.
(Shocher Tov 59:1)

Michal said, "The king of Israel uncovered himself today . . . as one of the worthless people reveals himself."
(2 Sam. 6:20)

Michal said to David, "Those of my father's house were extremely modest, whereas you stand and reveal yourself like one of the worthless ones."
(Bamidbar Rabbah 4:20)

"The five sons of Michal, daughter of Saul, whom she bore to Adriel" (2 Sam. 21:8). Merab bore them, and since Michal raised them, they are called Michal's children.
(Sanhedrin 19b)

꒰ꕤ꒱

*A*lthough princes and princesses of royal families are formally trained to obey the dictates of the kingdom, the pressures of that constricted existence have often, historically, led to emotional and internal strife within the courtly realm. This is as verifiable today as it was in the time of Israel's first monarchy.

Michal may have been a first-generation blue blood, but she acted as if her ancestors in Egypt had dined with Pharaohs instead of being employed as slaves in the construction of chic Egyptian "high-rises" (pyramids) along the Nile. This contrasts to her father Saul, who was, at the outset of his vocation, a restrained, good, and humble man.

Unfortunately for Michal, Jonathan, David, and her other family associates, Saul's evolving neuroses put everything, including Michal's filial loyalty, at risk. In addition, Michal does not properly estimate her own emotional vulnerability, particularly with regard to the young David. Her love for and loyalty to the young prince, who had no royal sophistication or training, cause her to disobey her father and bring her little joy and fulfillment. Although she supplanted her older sister, Merab, to win David's favor, the *shidduch* is more political than romantic in Saul's eyes. Later, David reveals his own political intentions, as he "redeems" Michal from Paltiel, her first husband, in an attempt to unite the northern kingdom of Israel with the southern kingdom of Judah. It is also clear, through David's other affaires of state, that Michal is not the principal passion of his life.

So Michal suffers. But she maintains her royal dignity throughout, chastising the unregal behavior of her husband as he dances triumphantly but vulgarly before the procession returning the ark to Jerusalem. Is she punished for daring to chastise the behavior of the prodigal son? The biblical text first records her infertility (2 Sam. 6:23) but later describes her as the mother of the five sons of her sister, Merab (2 Sam. 21:8). Michal, princess and mother of our people.

~~

Abigail

There were four exceptionally beautiful women in the world: Sarah, Rahab, Abigail, and Esther.

(Megillah 15a)

~~

"*H*e (a Jewish king) shall not take many wives" (Deut. 17:17)—even if they are as righteous as Abigail.

"Remember your maidservant" (1 Sam. 25:31). Abigail degraded herself by hinting to David that he should marry her. Because she did so, the verse diminished her name by one letter as it is written: "Then David said to *Abigal* (without the *yod*) (*Yerushalmi Sanhedrin* 2:3).

That beautiful women are the objects of men's desire is an age-old axiom. That their lives are blessed and happy because of their beauty is a patent falsehood. Such is the paradigm evinced in the single chapter narrative of Abigail, Nabal, and David.

She should have paid more attention to his name! Nabal means "wicked," "godless," "a vile person." Unfortunately, the biblical Nabal lives up to all these epithets. When David asks the "churlish" shepherd to lodge and feed his servants during their sojourn in Carmel, Nabal arrogantly refuses. The king is not pleased and prepares for war.

Abigail sallies forth, running to do a *mitzvah*, and offers a meal "fit for a king" that has been "down-loaded" on donkeys from atop Mount Carmel. The sheep, the loaves of bread, the wine, corn, raisins, and figs do not assuage David's wrath. But Abigail speaks forthrightly and imploringly and with brutal honesty about the baseness of her husband and stays the king's hand from bloodshed. It is a noble passage, flowing with self-sacrifice and political awareness. (Abigail has not survived all these years with an evil spouse by accident.) At the end, however, Abigail tips her hand, saying, "And when the Lord shall have dealt well with my lord, then remember thy handmaid" (1 Sam. 25:31).

This draws the attention of the commentators who correctly note that Abigail's name is immediately abbreviated to *Abigal*, a sign of dishonor. But "dear Abby" can live without the *yod*. Having received David's blessing, she returns to the ignorant and besotted Nabal, whom God smites after an appropriate ten-day period of possible repentance. The reward, both for sparing David from the sin of bloodshed and for her goodness, is immediate. She is summoned to the king to become his wife. *Abigal's* reaction? "Behold, thy handmaid is a servant to wash the feet of the servants of my lord" (1 Sam. 25:41). This is almost too humble to believe, especially when one considers *Abigal's* earlier machinations. Whatever her motivation, from this time forward, all her "hostessing" takes place in the king's palace.

❧

Nathan

Gad the seer and Nathan the prophet planned the construction of the Temple with David.

(*Seder Olam Rabbah* 20)

David sent messengers after Nathan to find out whether he was publicizing the matter of Bathsheba. Had he publicized it, David would have killed him.

(*Yalkut HaMechiri*, Ps. 51:19)

❧

"*A*nd Nathan said to David, 'Thou art the man'" (2 Sam. 12:7). Today Nathan's words to David would punctuate one's machismo. In the days of prophets and kings, it is one of the most damning statements in all of Scripture. Nathan excoriates King David for his wicked treatment of his loyal servant, Uriah the Hittite, the husband of the comely Bathsheba. Having sinned with his wife, David conspired with his general, Joab, to send the faithful but naive Uriah into the heat of battle where predictably he was slain.

The matter "displeased the Lord" (2 Sam. 11:27). Since Nathan the prophet was the Lord's representative, it also displeased him. In a strikingly efficient parable (more in the style of the New Testament) Nathan relates a story of a wealthy herdsman who took advantage of a poor man, robbing him of the "one little ewe lamb which he had bought and reared" (2 Sam. 12:3). David is greatly disturbed by the narrative, which must have appealed to his senses (and his former occupation) rather than his intellect, since the meaning of the pericope was transparent. Like one of Jesus's disciples in the book of Mark, he is disabused of his innocence by the angry and unforgiving Nathan.

The prophecy and the prophet are unrelenting. Nathan declares, "Now therefore, the sword shall never depart from thy house; because thou hast despised Me, and hast taken the wife of Uriah the Hittite to be thy wife. Thus saith the Lord: Behold, I will raise up evil against thee out of thine own house. . . ." (2 Sam. 12: 10–11).

David is repentant, but the die has been cast. External and internal troubles grieve his house. The child of David and Bathsheba's infamous tryst is born to a brief life of illness and suffering. David mourns and fasts throughout this excruciating period. When the child dies, the king, a new wisdom gained from his suffering, arises and regains his regal glory. Comforting his bathing beauty, he and Bathsheba are rewarded with the birth of the brilliant Solomon, whom the Lord loves.

And Nathan? New times, new prophetic blessings. Attending the *Brit*, he calls the newborn king Jedidah, "beloved of the Lord" (2 Sam. 12:25). He had spoken out on behalf of righteousness and still managed to keep his job in the firm.

ᘺ

Abner and Joab

Abner was punished because he made sport of the life of youths, because he put his own name before David's, and because he did not let Saul reconcile with David.

(*Yerushalmi Peah* 1:1)

They brought Joab to judgment and asked him, "Why did you kill Abner?" He replied, "I was the blood redeemer for Asahel."

(*Sanhedrin* 49a)

Joab was a sage, the head of the Sanhedrin, a great Torah scholar, and a mighty warrior.

(*Pesikta Rabbati* 11:50)

ᘺ

*T*he enmity Esau retained for his favored twin brother, Jacob, pales in comparison to the struggle waged between Joab and Abner. Of course, by the time of Israel's monarchy, the world had become much more complicated. Intrafamilial conflict had been replaced by political striving and divided kingdoms. Abner, the captain of Saul's army in the northern kingdom of Israel, is pitted against Joab, the general of David in the southern kingdom of Judah.

Joab seems to possess the markings of Jewish greatness. In addition to his field leadership, he is learned in Torah and loyal to David. After conquering the Ammonites at Rabbah, Joab sends messengers to David saying, "Encamp against the city, and take it; lest I take the city, and it be called after my name" (2 Sam. 12:28). Duly loyal yet, like every human being, possessor of a fatal flaw: he takes too much upon himself. Matters that are the province of the king of Israel, as well as the King of Israel, are executed by the zealous commander, first dutifully, then sinfully.

Abner is a slippery but less elusive personality than his biblical adversary. Always political, always manipulative, he supports whoever "seems" to be ascending to higher office. That could be Saul, Ish-bosheth, or David, and indeed all three receive his well-oiled ministrations. Abner is successful except for one critical error of judgment. He kills Joab's brother Asahel and enrages Joab, who exacts his revenge at the gates of Hebron. Unfortunately David, who has been persuaded by the sincerity of Abner's unctions, takes the killing personally but, like the Godfather, waits a generation to carry out the sentence.

In that period Joab, still David's general but acting more like Lawrence of Arabia in his psychotic phase, kills the forlorn Absalom (David's son) and then Amasa (Absalom's general). After David's death, he supports the candidacy of Adonijah as the king's successor. Solomon wins out, and Joab is slain at the altar of the Tent of the Lord. The end is more than ironic. For all his loyalty to the throne Joab is perceived, finally, as a traitor. Solomon delivers the epitaph: "The Lord will return Joab's blood upon his own head, because he fell upon two men more righteous and better than he [Abner and Amasa]. . . . So shall their blood return upon the head of Joab, and upon the head of his seed for ever" (1 Kings 2:32–33).

The prophet Samuel had warned the Israelites about the dangers of a monarchy (1 Sam. 8). Despite the noblest of efforts, his dire predictions had come home to roost.

Bathsheba

Bathsheba was destined to marry David since the six days of Creation, but she came to him in a painful manner.

(Sanhedrin 107a)

"And his wife you have taken to be your wife" (2 Sam. 12:9). "You are legally married to her."

(Shabbat 56a)

David the shepherd, David the slayer of the Philistine Goliath, Israel's greatest adversary, David the poet, David the king of his people possessed *midot*, wondrous Jewish attributes. Unfortunately, as the prescient Samuel had already announced, the monarchy, by replacing the theocracy with the rule of man, corrupted the souls of even the best leaders. As Saul succumbed to the pressures of the throne, so too did David lose himself in the pursuit of royal perquisites.

This led to sin and shame, and no amount of rabbinical eisegesis can erase the sin and shame that permeate the narrative of David and Bathsheba. He saw her "up on the roof." A woman, fair to look upon, performing her nightly ablutions. He saw, he sent, he sinned with the beautiful wife of Uriah the Hittite, David's faithful soldier. Bathsheba becomes pregnant, and loyal Uriah is, with the complicity of David's commander, Joab, done away with at the front lines of battle.

It is an ignominious episode, and its conclusion is handled better biblically than rabbinically. Bathsheba bears David a son, but the king is warned by his adviser and prophet, Nathan, that the child will bear the imprint of his father's guilt and die for his sins. In one of the most poignant passages of the Bible (2 Sam. 12:15–23), the agony of David and Bathsheba's grief is depicted. Yet "joy cometh in the morning." The Lord forgives his favored servant, and Bathsheba becomes the mother of one of Israel's greatest kings, renowned for his literary flair, his wit, and his inestimable wisdom. This is Solomon, whose name is derived from *shalom*, an appropriate appellation as Divinity takes steps (as He had done generations earlier by sending the dove to Noah as a coda to His anger) to restore the relationship between Himself and His people.

And Bathsheba? Certainly her *yichus*, her rightful place in Israel's royal history, is legitimatized and assured through the birth of the wise Solomon. She gives birth to three lesser-known sons as well (1 Chron. 3:5). Immortalized biblically, she becomes as prominent iconographically. Paintings by Hans Memling, Lucas Cranach, Rubens, Rembrandt, and Poussin render different poses of the Bible's greatest poseur. Her visage is, in the lyrics of Nat King Cole, "unforgettable."

Absalom

Because Absalom was vainglorious about his hair, he was hanged by it.

(*Sotah* 9b)

Absalom has no share in the World to Come.

(*Sanhedrin* 103b)

He deceived the hearts of three: his father, the court, and Israel. Therefore, three darts were thrust into his heart.

(*Sotah* 9b)

*A*s suggested earlier, the advent of the monarchy brought neither happiness nor fulfillment into the lives of Israel's leaders and their families. There was pain and anguish in the court of Saul, travail and mourning in the house of David. Indeed David, the sensitive soul, the national poet of Israel, endured more suffering than any other biblical figure, excluding the ineffable life of Job. David suffered but he could also dish out suffering, sometimes brutally, as in the case of Uriah the Hittite.

Amidst the raging struggle for power and supremacy between Saul (king of the northern realm of Israel) and David (leader of the southern kingdom of Judah) stood soldiers, advisers, sons, and daughters who took sides for political, romantic, or personal reasons. Absalom, son of David and Maacah, joined the fray; unfortunately, in the process he lost his place not only in this world but also in the World to Come. This began when, in a fit of righteous pique, he killed his half-brother Amnon, who had dishonored his full sister Tamar.

If this had been all, Absalom could probably have survived, but he suffered from an acute case of blind ambition. Trying to secure his position as David's successor, and fearing the candidacy of David and Bathsheba's newest and most brilliant prodigy, Solomon, he centralized his forces at Hebron and prepared a revolt against his father. In the resulting battle in Transjordan, Absalom's tribal combatants were outmatched by David's veteran army forces.

This could have been enough, but the Bible exacts a symbolically gruesome punishment. Riding on his mule (à la the future messiah of the New Testament), Absalom is accidentally raised up to the scaffold of a great terebinth, his head and glorious Nazirite hair caught in the tree's thick boughs (2 Sam. 18:9). Affixed to this biblical version of the cross, Absalom's shame is pierced by three "heart-directed" darts of David's general, Joab. It is too much for David who, having already mourned the death of an infant son (for whose death he bore direct responsibility), laments the loss of his oldest, wayward child: "O my son Absalom, my son, my son Absalom! Would I had died for thee, O Absalom, my son, my son!" The wailing continues until Joab reminds the king that Absalom was an adversary and that prolonged mourning over him would endanger the support of his own troops.

Nearly three millennia later William Faulkner would reformulate this story through the complex and tortuous narrative *Absalom, Absalom!* Faulkner depicted what the Bible had already revealed: the decay, tragedy, unfulfilled passion, and fury of David's House of Israel became a vision of the ruin of the South.

Solomon

All of Solomon's deeds were threefold. He had three ascents (in which the scope of his rulership increased until he ruled the whole world) and three declines (in which the scope of his rulership decreased until he ruled just over his household). He saw three worlds (having viewed life as a king, a commoner, and then again as a king). He committed three sins (having accumulated many horses, many wives, and much wealth). He wrote three books (Proverbs, Ecclesiastes, and The Song of Songs).
(*Shir HaShirim Rabbah* 1:10)

*T*o come close to an understanding of Solomon, son of David and Bathsheba, is to appreciate a multifaceted personality who experienced the very extremes of existence. Builder of the Jerusalem Temple, king, poet, historian, statesman, literatus, politician, philosopher, romantic, sage—Solomon was an exemplar for all that was good, wise, and superfluous in the history of Israel.

How to delimit a man who could create the eternal beauty of the book of Proverbs, the gentle cynicism of Ecclesiastes, the sensual rhythms of The Song of Songs? Solomon could not be,

would not be, confined or defined as any type of biblical hero.
He shattered every paradigm in every aspect of his life. A child
born out of wedlock to the Lord's most favored shepherd and the
"unforgettable" Bathsheba, he embodied the poetic, musical lilt
of his father as well as the aristocratic, unmoved, yet seductive
beauty of his mother. Possessor of a thousand wives (including
the Queen of Sheba), ruler over 252 provinces, a judge of unpar-
alleled wisdom, a man of war and peace, a student and expounder
of Torah, a royal monarch who reveled in the golden perquisites
of office—when Solomon moved, the earth shook.

Yes, this was a giant of our people, somewhat infantilized by
Isaac Rosenfeld's delightful fantasy of Solomon's dotage (*King
Solomon*, 1956). He had everything, he had nothing, if that indeed is the explicit message of Ecclesiastes in brief. He was a man
of excess in everything he assayed. As Aristotle had once perceived
the author of creation as the "Unmoved Mover," so too did
Solomon's creative gifts overflow, although he remained unmoved.
To know him was to love him but, as Rosenfeld neatly suggests,
a man of this breadth, who seemingly possessed the key to all
forms of worldly and spiritual knowledge, could not really love in
return. He was the ultimate narcissist, creating beauty by his very
presence, which enlightened and stimulated all who were lucky
enough to receive his attention. Yet somehow there remained a
penumbra of coldness, an aloofness that surrounded and protected
the brilliant king and survived his earthly career.

Yet he is described in this way:

> And God gave Solomon wisdom and understanding exceeding
> much, and largeness of heart, even as the sand that is on the sea-
> shore. And Solomon's wisdom excelled the wisdom of all the chil-
> dren of the east, and all the wisdom of Egypt. And there came of
> all peoples to hear the wisdom of Solomon, from all kings of the
> earth, who had heard of his wisdom.
>
> (1 Kings 5:9–10,14)

Solomon, our sage, our soothsayer, our resplendent, impetuous,
inexplicable king.

Hiram

When greatness was given to Hiram king of Tyre, he said, "I am a god, I sit in the seat of God" (Ezek. 28:2).

(*Chullin* 89a)

With wisdom, Hiram built himself a palace between the Adriatic Sea and the Mediterranean.

(*Tanchuma Bereishit*)

Scholars often describe Judaism as a syncretic tradition. That is, our people and their leaders survived and prospered by absorbing and assimilating the "affects" of other cultures. This societal pattern was already in place 1,000 years before the Common Era. At that time King Solomon sent to Hiram asking for his aid in building the Jerusalem Temple.

(1 Kings 5:15–32)

*L*ike Solomon, Hiram was a man of enormous talents and had an ego to boot. He was the King of Tyre, a contemporary of David and Solomon, the Robert Moses of his day. He had the mind of a city planner and the power to effect his designs. During Hiram's reign, Tyre became the cynosure of Phoenician art, architecture, and culture. It was only natural that Solomon would seek his counsel. Hiram had already built many temples to the gods; surely he could assist in erecting The Temple to the One God.

An alliance was formed through correspondence that is cited biblically and confirmed in the writings of Josephus. Cedarwood from Lebanon and skilled Tyrian construction workers were lent to Solomon's project in exchange for wheat and oil, and mercantile concessions were made for a king who wanted to aggrandize his nation's naval reputation. "And there was peace between Hiram and Solomon; and they two made a league together" (1 Kings 5:26).

So, as in most political transactions, there was measure for measure. Solomon sent 30,000 men to Lebanon to help hew the wood, quarry the stones, and thus prepare, with Hiram acting as consultant, the foundation of the temple. It was a relationship that spanned two generations. Hiram had sent cedar trees, carpenters, and masons earlier to David in order to build him a house (2 Sam. 5:11). The construction of the temple was a product of that earlier alliance.

Interestingly, the significance of this contractual relationship between the two kingdoms is diminished by our sages' contemptuous characterization of Hiram, a non-Jew, as the ultimate egoist. Considering the size of the personalities on the other side of this alliance (David and Solomon), one wonders what the rabbis found so egregious in Hiram's behavior. In the biblical context, and in their realpolitik approach to life, Hiram and the kings of Israel were a perfect match.

David

David was Israel's shepherd, as it is written: "You shall shepherd My people Israel."

(2 Sam. 5:2)

The most praiseworthy king was David. The most praiseworthy prophet was Moses. Whatever Moses did, David did. Moses took Israel out of Egypt; David took Israel out of the subjugation of the kingdoms. Moses waged war, and David waged war. Moses was king of Israel and Judah, and David was king of Israel and Judah. Moses split the sea for Israel, and David split the rivers for Israel. Moses erected an altar, and David erected an altar. Moses sacrificed and David sacrificed. Moses gave Israel the five books of Torah, and David gave Israel the five books that constitute Psalms.

(*Shocher Tov* 1:2)

If you study David, you will find in him no sin other than the one with Uriah.

(*Shabbat* 56a)

Said David before the Holy One, Blessed is He: "Master of the Universe, despise not my prayer, for Israel's eyes are raised to me in hope, and my eyes are raised to you in hope. If You hear my prayer, it is as if You heard theirs."

(*Shocher Tov* 25:5)

"Behold, I have seen a son of Jesse the Bethlehemite, that is skillful in playing, and a mighty man of valor, and a man of war, and prudent in affairs, and
a comely person, and the Lord is with him" (1 Sam. 16:18). "Skillful
in playing"—in understanding Scripture; "a mighty man of valor"—in Mishnah;
"a man of war"—who knows how to give and take in the battle of Torah discussion; "prudent in affairs"—in good deeds; "a comely person"—in Talmud.
(*Ruth Rabbah* 4:3)

David composed 120 psalms but ended none of them with "hallelujah"
until he foresaw the downfall of the wicked.
(*Vayikra Rabbah* 4:7)

These are the two anointed ones, who stand by the Lord of the whole earth"
(Zech. 4:14). These are Aaron and David, who were anointed with the oil
of anointment. Aaron received the priesthood; David, the kingship.
(*Bamidbar Rabbah* 18:16)

$\mathcal{T}$ here are a few historical figures who, through their life, gar-
ner such exalted reputations that they become part of the myth
and mythos of humanity as well as the central figure of world re-
ligions. The two transcendent figures of the Hebrew Bible are
Moses and David. But David, at least in the eyes of Christianity,
climbs to an even higher rung of honor, as the book of Matthew
traces the genealogy of Jesus through the great king of Israel.

This is no accident. David, one of the most complicated characters to grace the pages of Scripture, fulfilled many messianic
expectations of the Hebrew people, and since the New Testament
authors viewed their Scripture as the fulfillment of the Old Testament, it was natural to attach the "new messiah" to the "old."

And why not? What better preparation for messiahship than
an internship as shepherd? The rest of David's résumé was blank,
but his humility and faith in the God of his ancestors reached the
gates of heaven. A singer of psalms, a musician, the young David
(perfectly carved and perfectly represented in Michelangelo's
statuary) had no other conceptions about war, politics, women,
architecture, nation building, and statesmanship. That he acquired very vivid conceptions of all the preceding gives evidence
to his extraordinary acumen, but the resultant loss of faith and
humility remains one of the great biblical tragedies.

Yet he is almost always viewed as Israel's hero, despite his frailties, and notwithstanding his immoral and unforgivable disposal of Uriah the Hittite. David will always be associated with the slaying of the inimical Goliath and the concomitant inspiration of Saul's armies. His love of Jonathan, perfectly reciprocated, is also his legacy. The extent of their intimacy has been speculated upon, but one must be careful not to read the ultraliberal mores of the late twentieth century into the biblical world. David's love of women, particularly his attraction to Bathsheba, which both ruined and resurrected the king, reveals the unbridled, instinctive nature of a man who placed his passions even above the law. His passionate love of his children, his desperate attempt to keep the rebellious Absalom in the fold, provide the most intimate, sentimental, and heartrending portraits in Scripture.

He began his reign reluctantly. Perhaps he knew too well that Samuel's warning about the corruption of kingship was a fatal prophecy. As a boy, he watched with terror the deterioration of the once humble Saul, whom he tried to placate with the gentle rhythms of his lyre and his paeans to the God of Israel. But something of Saul—or was it Saul's office?—rubbed off on the brilliant protégé. David became dizzy with success and overwrought with failure. His life lust was boundless. He danced a brazen half-naked dance before the Ark of the Covenant as it was being brought to Jerusalem. He fought with fury, judged his people with intense scrutiny and fairness, and sought the Lord's forgiveness of his sins with the utmost devotion and fervent prayers.

He may be the most human, the most touchable, the most sensitive of all our biblical heroes. Moses was aloof; Solomon was narcissistic; only Abraham's humanity was as patent, but still the portrait of David is more vivid, more complete. He knows and is known. He is at times uncomfortable that his life is lived so publicly, but finally, it is clear, he would have had it no other way. David our shepherd, our poet, our prophet, our sage.

Elijah the Tishbite

Why was Elijah privileged to be able to revive the dead? Because he did the will of the Holy One, Blessed is He, and he would sigh over the honor of Israel every day as if Israel were in danger of being destroyed from the world. In every generation that Elijah found righteous men, he would embrace and kiss them and bless the Holy One.

(Tanna d'Bei Eliyahu Rabbah 5:11)

"The son of the woman, the mistress of the house, fell sick" (1 Kings 17:17). Elijah prayed that he be given the key to resurrection of the dead. He was answered: "There are three keys that were not given to any messenger: the keys to childbirth, to rain, and to resurrection of the dead. I have given you the key to rain, and now you ask for the key to resurrection? People will say, 'Two keys are in the hands of the disciple, and only one in the hands of the master. Bring back the key for rain that is in your hand and take the other.'"

(Sanhedrin 113a)

Ten things were created on the eve of the Sabbath at twilight. One of them was the cave in Sinai in which Moses and later Elijah stood.

(Pesachim 54a)

Elijah still lives.

(Seder Olam Rabbah 1)

⨯

*P*erhaps more than any of the glorious personalities depicted in the Bible, Elijah the Prophet has transcended Jewish history and Jewish time. At the most dramatic moment of the Passover Seder the door is opened for Elijah, the "cup of Elijah" is symbolically raised, and the messianic strains of *"Eliyahu Hanavi"* are intoned, thus revealing a deep and age-old Jewish belief in the coming of the messiah. Elijah is welcomed at every circumcision ceremony, where we do not have a *kos Eliyahu* (Elijah's cup) but a *kisei Eliyahu* (Elijah's chair). He graces many midrashim, stories, and narratives—often in mufti—where he performs acts of kindness and redemption. On Shabbat Hagadol, the Sabbath preceding Passover, his name is invoked in the Haftarah lection: "Behold, I will send you Elijah the prophet before the coming of the great and terrible day of the Lord" (Mal. 3:24).

This messianic, sometimes cloyingly sentimental presence drops in and out of our Jewish lives. He is our gift of redemption; he remains a religious and historical problem. That is, how to reconcile Elijah's biblical and rabbinical destiny with the evolution of the Gospel and New Testament tradition? Elijah may appear to be a second Moses; the first redeemed us from Egypt, the second represented the redemption in the world to come. However, as the world turned and words like "apocalypse" and "messiah" entered the vocabulary of late antiquity, he began to look more like a prefigurement of John the Baptist or the Christian savior. Emerging from the wilderness, Elijah is described as "a hairy man, girt with a girdle of leather about his loins" (2 Kings 1:8), preaching a doctrine of return and repentance before the God of Israel.

The biblical Elijah, interestingly, seems devoid of sentimentality. He accepts his prophetic mission piously, first with a small act of loving kindness to a widow, later exacting punishment upon Ahab and Jezebel's false prophets of Ba'al. The brutality of the punishment is rivaled by Elijah's powers over nature. He brings forth the rain and resurrects the dead in a parable redolent of the

New Testament (1 Kings 17:17–24). He travels forty days in the desert, like Moses, to receive God's testimony on Mount Horeb. There, after experiencing the power of the Lord's natural forces (earthquakes, wind, and fire), Elijah hears a "still small voice." His response is one of acceptance and lament: "I, even I only, am left; and they seek my life to take it away" (1 Kings 19:14).

Finally the reader witnesses Elijah's exquisite departure from his earthly career. As his protégé and successor Elisha watches, "a chariot of fire and horses of fire" whisk the uncompromising prophet heavenward (2 Kings 2:11). The loyal Elisha literally takes up Elijah's mantle and continues the miraculous performance.

Miracles, resurrection, fiery endings. The religion of the early prophets and the Torah was being challenged by these new leaders. Elijah the Tishbite came from the tradition of Moses, but by the time his chariot traced a fiery arc in the sky, he had created a new vision of Israelite history. Yet Elijah would have been disturbed to learn that his narrative served the literary and philosophical aims of the authors of the New Testament. He viewed himself, finally, as a *Ben Adam*—one of our people.

Despite his being "borrowed" by a new tradition, Elijah remains, in his rabbinical garment, one of our most beloved and cherished personalities. *Eliyahu Hanavi.*

꒲

Ahab and Jezebel

Ahab took the vineyard of Naboth lawfully. However, he was punished for killing Naboth without trial.

(*Zohar* 1:192b)

He inscribed on the gates of Samaria: "Ahab has denied the God of Israel."

(*Sanhedrin* 102b)

The account of Ahab was balanced; his *mitzvot* equaled his sins. He was generous with his money, and because he benefited Torah scholars with his wealth, half of his transgressions were forgiven.

(*Sanhedrin* 102b)

It is not to the benefit of the wicked that they are shown favor in this world. It was not to Ahab's benefit that he was shown favor in This World, as it is written: "Because he humbles himself before Me" (1 Kings 21:29). The sins Ahab committed during the extra time he was granted on earth caused him to lose his share in the World to Come.

(*Maharsha, Yoma* 87a)

Who caused Ahab to be destroyed in this world and the world to come together with his sons? His wife Jezebel.

(*Tanna d'Bei Eliyahu Rabbah* 10)

꒲

"*A*nd Ahab the son of Omri reigned over Israel in Samaria twenty and two years. And Ahab the son of Omri did that which was evil in the sight of the Lord above all that were before him" (1 Kings 16:29–30). So begins the tragic narrative of Ahab.

It could have been better. This was a skilled warrior, an astute politician, a clever businessman, and a lover of Torah. Unfortunately, not every lover of Torah has felt compelled to practice all the *mitzvot*. The son of Omri was interested in the security and aggrandizement of Israel, but somewhere amidst his alliance with Judah, his exchange of trade with the Tyrians, his building of a grand stable at Megiddo, his three wars against Ben-Hadad, king of Damascus, and his union with Syria against the Assyrians he lost his way.

It is easy to blame Jezebel, another character whose name has been continually vilified through the pages of literature and history. But her destiny was more deserving. Certainly she had the king's ear and his heart, and that proved to be a deadly combination. That she succeeded in her ungodly plan to annex Naboth's vineyard to her husband's land and, at the same time, destroy the poor farmer underlines her venality. It doesn't say a lot for Ahab either, but at least, after being rebuked by a furious Elijah, he possessed enough shame to return to his palace and put on a mourner's sackcloth.

The counts against him: false prophets of Ba'al, a Phoenician wife, sinful behavior against his fellow man. Ahab didn't have a chance to win favor in the Lord's eyes. His fate sealed, the beleaguered king makes one more attempt to avenge himself in battle. Disguised as a foot soldier, he is killed by the Arameans. And, as predicted earlier by Elijah, his blood is ingloriously licked up by dogs in Samaria.

Was there a white whale looming over the biblical Ahab? Certainly he was obsessed with the simultaneous occupation of proving and redeeming himself. That he failed tragically in his quest to right his ship of state earns not just our enmity but, like our study of Melville's Ahab, our continuous intrigue with this enormously complex biblical personality.

Isaiah

The Holy One, Blessed is He, said to Isaiah, "My children are troublesome and rebellious. If you undertake to be hit and degraded by My children, you will go on My mission; otherwise you will not." Isaiah replied, "I accept the condition and I am not worthy of going on a mission to Your children." Then the Holy One said, "All the prophets received the spirit of prophecies from another prophet, but you will receive your prophecies from the mouth of the Lord. All the prophets prophesied simple prophecies, but you will prophesy double comforts: be comforted, be comforted" (Isa. 40:1).

(Vayikra Rabbah 10:2)

Isaiah prophesied many more prophecies than all the other prophets; moreover, he prophesied about all the nations of the world.

(Pesikta Rabbati 33:25)

Six hundred thirteen precepts were told to Moses on Mount Sinai. Isaiah came and stressed six principles.

(Makkot 24a)

The Lord said, "No one loves My children more than Isaiah."

(Yalkut Hamechiri, Mishlei 30:10)

The people of Israel said to Isaiah, "Our teacher, perhaps you have come to comfort only the generation in whose days the Temple was destroyed." He replied, "I have come to comfort all generations."

(Pesikta d'Rav Kahana 16:103)

⌒

*T*he call of God brought forth from his chosen prophets a typical response: Who are we to serve the Almighty in truth? The characteristic of humility in Abraham, in Moses, and now in Isaiah was a prerequisite for service. When one considers the rigors of their prophetic careers, and Divinity's imperative to stand up against injustice, corruption, and sinfulness, he might wonder if humility were truly the most important attribute possessed by a potential leader of the people.

It certainly wouldn't work that way today. "Ambitious," "aggressive," and "fearless" are modern watchwords of success, which causes one to pause. Why, in the ancient world, was humility considered an essential part of leadership? Perhaps because the humble person was more comprehending and more responsive to a force in life much greater than himself. This does not mean he suppressed his personality and his talents, but rather he saw himself in proper perspective: merely a vessel of God's desires for His people.

This selfless approach takes nothing away from the majestic reach of his career. There was no prophet more majestic in language, thought, or historical purpose. Isaiah "saw" everything—the present and future history of Israel, the present and future history of humankind. There is no book[1] more eloquent, quoted, or more focused on the particulars of Israel's role in the world, or more concerned with the Lord's message to all the peoples of the earth. Isaiah, indeed, was a "light to the nations."

He excoriated Israel for sinful behavior. This ability to chastise had always been a function of the *gedolei hador* (the leaders of the generation). Isaiah insisted that there was a causal connection between Israel's sins and her eventual defeat and exile at the hands of her adversaries. Whether this philosophical outlook is supportable is less relevant to the reader of Isaiah than the idea

---

1. It may be more accurate to speak of the "books" of Isaiah, since scholars posit Chapters 40 to 66 as second Isaiah.

that this prophet, poet, and homiletician extraordinaire placed ethical behavior above every other form of existence. Failure to relieve the oppressed, the widowed, the blind, the underprivileged, resulted in punishment. That punishment amounted, no less, to the destruction of the Jerusalem Temple and exile into gentile lands.

The message could not have been clearer, and yet the role of the prophet was to have his ineffable words disregarded and ignored. This reality, well known by God's indefatigable and unrelenting servants, only made the message more poignant and the punishment (which could have been avoided by true repentance) more frustrating. When the Assyrians besiege Samaria, the capital of the kingdom of Israel, the prophet explains the attack as a manifestation of God's anger against His chosen people.

Monarchal eras come and go. While the history of Israel, its sixth-century B.C.E. exile to Babylonia, and later return to the Promised Land are vital components to the understanding of our people's evolution, Isaiah's words continue to resonate in all our hearts as stepping stones toward true faith, justice, morality, and purity of religious existence. Invoked by religious leaders of all faiths, embraced by social movements, Isaiah's message is timeless and remains, remarkably, timely.

The greatest novel in the history of American-Jewish literature, Henry Roth's *Call It Sleep* (1934), employs Isaiah's vision of his dramatic encounter in the Temple with the Lord and the seraphim (Isa. 6). This depiction of the Lord of Hosts, articulated and internalized by the precocious child David Schearl, becomes the text and context for his own mission: his fantastic physical, intellectual, and prophetic journey through the teeming immigrant streets of New York.

> Holy, holy, holy, is the Lord of hosts;
> The whole earth is full of his glory.
> (Isa. 6:3)

Imbedded in our liturgy, in our hearts, the words of Isaiah are often too precious too bear, too difficult to live up to, but most of all, too unbearable to live without.

୬

Cyrus

Cyrus wept and groaned over the Temple's destruction.

(*Seder Eliyahu Rabbah* 19)

Cyrus said, "He is the God who is in Jerusalem" (Ezra 1:3), for although the city is desolate, God does not move from it.

(*Shemot Rabbah* 2:2)

୬

*I*f Hiram, the king of Tyre, deserves a place among Israel's luminous personalities, how much more so Cyrus? The prophet Isaiah pays tribute to the Persian king who in 539 B.C.E., after his defeat of the Babylonians, allows the Jewish exiles to return to Jerusalem and rebuild their Temple. Isaiah, citing the Lord, asserts:

> Cyrus is my shepherd,
> And shall perform all My pleasure;
> Even saying of Jerusalem: "She shall be built";
> And to the temple: "Thy foundation shall be laid."
>
> (Isa. 44:28)

And continues:

> Thus saith the Lord to His anointed,
> To Cyrus, whose right hand I have holden,
> To subdue nations before him. . . .
>
> (Isa. 45:1)

In the book of Ezra this messianic promise is made manifest:

> Thus saith Cyrus king of Persia: "All the kingdoms of the earth hath
> the Lord, the God of heaven, given me; and He hath charged me
> to build Him a house in Jerusalem, which is in Judah. Whosoever
> there is among you of all His people—his God be with him—let
> him go up to Jerusalem, which is in Judah, and build the house of
> the Lord, the God of Israel, He is the God who is in Jerusalem."
> (Ezra 1:2–3)

Yes, it is historically true that the Persian king employed a policy
of restoration with the defeated Babylonians as well, allowing them
to rebuild their temples and reestablish their cults. Notwithstanding his ulterior motive (if any), he clearly performed a great *mitzvah*
for the Jewish people. In an age wherein the righteous gentile is
extolled and glorified, King Cyrus most certainly has earned his
"day in God's celestial court."

~3~

Jeremiah

"Cursed be the day on which I was born" (Jer. 20:14), the ninth of Av.

(*Midrash Iyov*, Wertheimer 20)

Jeremiah, son of Hilkiah, prophesied close to the time of the destruction of the First Temple.

(*Seder Olam Rabbah* 20)

Jeremiah wrote his book, Jeremiah, the book of Kings, and Lamentations.

(*Bava Batra* 15a)

The prophets who prophesied during the First Temple would conclude with words of praise and comfort—except for Jeremiah, who concluded with words of rebuke.

(*Yerushalmi Berachot* 5:1)

"Master of the world," said Jeremiah, "what sins were in my hands that of all the prophets who arose before me and who will arise after me, You destroyed Your temple through none but me?" God replied, "Before I created the world, you were designated for that."

(*Pesikta Rabbati* 27:5)

Three prophets prophesied with the word *eichah* ("how"): Moses, Isaiah, and Jeremiah. Jeremiah, who beheld the Jews in their disgrace, said, "How does she sit in solitude!" (Lam. 1:1).

(*Eichah Rabbati* 1:1)

Jeremiah never married, Israel's only prophet bereft of family. This was not his choice. On the contrary, it was a Divine prohibition! "Thou shalt not take thee a wife, neither shalt thou have sons or daughters in this place" (Jer. 16:2). Whereas other religious traditions have extolled the monastic life, the teachers of Judaism have always emphasized the Genesis commandment: "Be fruitful and multiply."

(Gen. 1:28)

Not so Jeremiah. And this lack of spouse and family underlined his condition: he was alone; he was also lonely. Furthermore, in the tradition of the preceding prophets, he was shy: "Ah, Lord God! Behold, I cannot speak; for I am a child" (Jer. 1:6). But the mission was thrust upon him with an immediacy that was both alarming and intimidating, for it was Jeremiah who was to preside as Israel's prophet during the destruction of the Jerusalem Temple. The Lord said: "See, I have this day set thee over the nations and the kingdoms, to root out and to pull down, and to destroy and to overthrow; to build, and to plant.

(Jer. 1:10)

*A*t least Isaiah, in the latter part of his ministry, had the good fortune to offer his people *nechemta* (consolation) upon their travails in exile and their imminent return to Israel at the graceful hand of the Persian King Cyrus. Although Jeremiah's prophecies did include a few passages of consolation, in general they were darker than Isaiah's. Did this affect his personality? Would he have been happier to have served in another period in Israel's history? It is facile to answer the questions affirmatively, but neither response does justice to his book and his central role as a suffering servant of the Jewish people.

Yes, if one wants to underline "guilt" as an inherently Jewish characteristic, Jeremiah is the sourcebook. His birth on the ninth of Av confirms his status as our tradition's *kapparah* (expiatory sacrifice); that he is credited with writing the book of Lamentations, which is read on Tishah b'Av, confirms the intellectual and spiritual acceptance of his place in Jewish life. The brilliant literary critic and poet, Jacob Picard, hearkened back to the particular role of guilt assumed by Jeremiah in his short story "The Marked One" (1956). The protagonist, Sender Frank, tried to resist his fate of bearing his community's guilt but, as in the tribulations of the lamenting Jeremiah, he was forced to bear the unbearable.

This theme, though tragic, threads its way through the history of the prophets. Their words were unaccepted, their earthly existences threatened. Jeremiah, like Joseph, is thrown into a pit. Jeremiah is human; he is frail; he bemoans his fate. Yet he transcends his humanity for the sake of truth and emerges as one of Judaism's greatest symbols of endurance and faithfulness to the God of his ancestors.

It is this admixture of guilt, suffering, and standing-up for righteousness in the centuries succeeding Jeremiah's prophetic career that has been internalized by the Jewish people. That Jeremiah's internal anxieties qualified him as a good candidate for the psychiatrist's couch indicates the depth of our people's and our religion's struggle over how to live our lives. It has been a struggle not only over the choice between the external rewards and punishments of good and evil behavior, but over the internal person, who anguishes for himself and his neighbor, recognizing the pain of both, but learning the obligation to sacrifice for the good of his community. This is the stuff of martyrdom, a theme centralized in Christianity, but initiated and later pushed to the periphery of Judaism. It adheres to every sentence ascribed to our suffering prophet, Jeremiah, who "before he came forth from the womb was sanctified and appointed a prophet unto the nations" (Jer. 1:5).

Jeremiah, God's suffering servant, "the marked one" of our people.

Ezekiel

All that Ezekiel saw, Isaiah saw also. To what can Ezekiel be compared? To a villager who saw the king and is therefore awed by every detail that he sees. And to what can Isaiah be compared? To a city dweller who saw the king and is less awed. This explains why Ezekiel described his visions of the heavenly throne in much greater detail than did Isaiah.

(*Chagigah* 13b)

Ezekiel began to complain before the Holy One, Blessed is He: "Master of the Universe," he said, "Am I not a priest and a prophet? Why did Isaiah prophesy in Jerusalem, whereas I must prophesy in the exile?" Immediately, the Holy One opened before him the seven lower levels of heaven, and he looked at them and saw all that is above.

(*Batei Midrashot* 2:127)

Why did Ezekiel merit that the dead be resurrected through him? Because he felt a complete sense of identity with Israel.

(*Tanna d'Bei Eliyahu Rabbah* 5)

There are visions, and there are visions. The former tend, as in the time of Isaiah, to relate to the *Weltanschauung* ("world view") of the biblical period. Isaiah, despite his divergent ministries (one of chastisement, the other of comfort), possessed a regal dignity and an unmatched form of poetic expression. His book dwells on the highest level of the vast corpus of Jewish literature. Ezekiel is a different matter. This distinction is evidenced in popular culture's embrace of his vision of the valley of dry bones.

(Ezek. 37:1–14)

෴

*T*he midrash attributes Ezekiel's vision to his lack of sophistication. Indeed, Ezekiel compared to Isaiah was unsophisticated, but that is the equivalent of comparing the works of Herman Wouk to those of Saul Bellow! Ezekiel was, and remains, a formidable prophet. His writing reflects less a lack of sophistication than the time, the place, and conditions in which he wrote. Exiled Israel was seeking answers to its destiny, and as the depression caused by the exile grew greater, so did the literary flights of fancy.

It was fanciful but not without basis or reason. Radical theologies and philosophies began to burgeon in the Syrian Orient of late antiquity, and the Jews, intellectually and spiritually curious as always, were susceptible to the teachings of the Persians, Greeks, and Romans. Eschatology, the doctrine of death and final things, was not a focus of the patriarchal world; neither was the topic of resurrection. But through contact with these disparate ancient peoples and because of our own national crisis, foreign ideas, words, and religious concepts began to be assimilated.

And so came Ezekiel, startlingly, but not *ex nihilo*. He was stimulating, he was radical, and he was still Jewish! But his visions were, quite literally, out of this world. This begins with his first chapter in which the prophet receives the "call" from four four-faced creatures who are transported through the air in what seems to be an ancient version of a 4x4 vehicle. The visions, parables, and prophecies grow stranger from there, until Ezekiel dreams of his people's restoration to the land through the reassembling of their "dry bones."

It is not a narrative for the beginning student. The movement the book of Ezekiel spawned, *merkavah* (chariot) mysticism, led to great internal arguments over this prophet's place in the biblical canon. The controversy will always rage about this radical, innovative book, but at its heart remained a prophet of Israel committed to his people, the return to his homeland, and faith in his God. For a Jew suffering in the Diaspora, Ezekiel's message must have brought hope for eventual redemption.

~~

Hosea

All the prophets called upon Israel to repent, but not like Hosea. Jeremiah and Isaiah did not teach Israel what to say, whereas Hosea taught them how to appease God: "Say to Him, 'Forgive all iniquity. . . .'" (Hos. 14:3). In addition, he declared Israel to be merely stumblers, as it is written: "You have stumbled in your iniquity."

(Pesikta Rabbati 44:23)

The Holy One, Blessed is He, said to Reuben: "You were the first to repent. By your life, your descendant will be the first to urge repentance." This refers to Hosea, who said, "Return, O Israel" (Hos. 14:2).

(Bereishit Rabbah 84:19)

Compared to the love Moses expressed toward Israel and compared to the contempt Balaam expressed toward them, Hosea was neutral about Israel: he neither loved nor hated them.

(Bamidbar Rabbah 2:17)

~~

*I*t is the eighth century B.C.E. The Northern Kingdom of Israel is being threatened by the Assyrians and is on the verge of collapse. Hosea, the son of Be'eri, is chosen at the beginning of his ministry to show the sins and waywardness of the Jewish people

by marrying a harlot. Obediently, he follows the Divine imperative and marries Gomer. They have two sons, Jezreel and Lo-
Ammi, and a daughter, Lo-Ruhamah. The progeny have both
specific and symbolic destinies. Jezreel is to bring to an end the
kingdom of Jehu. Lo-Ruhamah, meaning "that hath not obtained
compassion," and Lo-Ammi, meaning "not my people," represent
the Lord's rejection of Israel.

There are sacrifices one makes in taking on the role of the
prophet. Jeremiah is denied a family. Hosea's role as submissive
husband is just as striking. In each case, however, the prophet's
misery and unhappiness are extended to his people. That is, our
people are seen through the career suffering of the prophet; it is
not the other way around.

This is in no way a mitigation of Israel's sins, which are neatly
enumerated and rehearsed by Hosea and his eleven prophetic
colleagues. It rather imparts more evidence of the biblical authors'
literary panache. Hosea was gifted. His brevity should not be
confused with his stature. He railed against Israel's infidelity, its
worship of Ba'al, and lamented the loss of worship of God. He
was stern, unbending, and yet, finally, he typifies Israel's prophet:
he offers consolation—the opportunity for Israel to repent and
receive God's favor and blessing once again. His words have particular significance in Judaism, for on the Sabbath of Repentance,
the Haftarah begins with Hosea 14:2:

> Return, O Israel, unto the Lord thy God;
> For thou hast stumbled in thine iniquity.

Hosea, sufferer for and against Israel, lover and chastiser of our
people.

꒒

Joel

Joel called the evil inclination "hidden" (Joel 2:20), for it hides in man's heart.

(*Sukkah* 52a)

꒒

*I*t is harder to approach some of the minor prophets than others. Hosea's and Jeremiah's lives are open; they bleed for our people. Joel, who seems to cull some of his verses from Isaiah (what better source of rebuke and comfort than that redoubtable sage?), speaks succinctly, poetically, typically, and tersely but not personally. After first depicting Israel's downfall, he turns to classical themes of repentance and redemption.

The first two chapters of Joel describe the Lord's devastation of nature through a plague of locusts. The prophet threatens the people: "For great is the day of the Lord and very terrible; and who can abide it?" (Joel 2:11). Yet suffering can be relieved if the people seek the Lord through sincere prayer and repentance. The reward is explicit:

> And it shall come to pass afterward,
> That I will pour out My spirit upon all flesh;
> And your sons and your daughters shall prophesy,
> Your old men shall dream dreams,
> Your young men shall see visions.   (Joel 3:1)

The symbolism and imagery are bold and distinct. Those who believe in the Lord will be redeemed as God destroys Israel's enemies. Four chapters of suffering and reward. The Lord ultimately returns to a repentant people, and when that day comes:

> The mountains shall drop down sweet wine,
> And the hills shall flow with milk
> And all the brooks of Judah shall flow with waters;
> And a fountain shall come forth of the house of the Lord.
>
> (Joel 4:18)

Amos

All the prophets were wealthy. Amos owned cattle and had sycamores in the lowlands.

(Nedarim 38a)

They called him "the stutterer" because he stuttered.

(Vayikra Rabbah 10:2)

Six hundred thirteen precepts were told to Moses at Sinai. Amos came and stressed one: "Seek Me and live."

(Amos 5:4) (Makkot 24a)

*H*e came with the classic prophetic credentials: humble origins and a fear of chastising his people. He tells Amaziah the priest: "I was no prophet, neither was I a prophet's son; but I was a herdsman, and a dresser of sycamore trees (Amos 7:14). And yet, when faced with the Divine challenge and mission, there was no prophet mightier or more powerful in his castigation of the people of Israel:

> The Lord roareth from Zion
> And uttereth His voice from Jerusalem;
> And the pastures of the shepherds shall mourn,
> And the top of Carmel shall wither.   (Amos 1:2).

Amos's visions of Israel's destruction are varied and potent. He was appalled by the class distinctions within urban culture and condemns, unmitigatingly, a society that has become fat, lazy, and idolatrous. These societal inequities would be resolved, adumbrates the prophet, by means of a two-pronged punishment of Israel executed by God and the nation of Assyria.

Amos's illustrations of God's plan are remarkably vivid. Locusts, fire, the razing of city walls, and the desecration of the altar are all pitted against the feeble plea of the prophet for the welfare of his people. Anticipating tragedy, Amos asks, "How shall Jacob stand, for he is small." The Lord answers, "It shall not be" (Amos 7:2–3).

Despite his humility, Amos rises to greatness in both tone and imagery. Chapter 3 is a small but great masterpiece as it describes not only the vocation of the prophet but the coming punishment and exile of his charges. Mixing agrarian and urban metaphor, Amos concludes this section describing the Lord's wrath against Israel:

> Thus saith the Lord:
> As the shepherd rescueth out of the mouth of the lion
> Two legs, or a piece of an ear,
> So shall the children of Israel that dwell in Samaria
> Escape with the corner of a couch, and the leg of a bed.
> (Amos 3:12)

The metaphors continue. Israel's imminent destruction is depicted through Hebrew assonance. "Summer fruit" (*kayitz*) becomes the *ketz*, end of Israel. The barrage of Amos's prophetic volleys thunders forth. Finally, with four verses remaining in the last chapter, Amos offers the typical prophetic comfort. The return to agronomy, a more pristine form of existence, is extolled profoundly by the shepherd:

> And they shall plant vineyards, and drink the wine thereof;
> They shall also make gardens, and eat the fruit of them
> And I will plant them upon their land,
> And they shall no more be plucked up
> Out of their land which I have given them,
> Saith the Lord thy God.   (Amos 9: 14–15).

This is Amos's prophecy; this is his prayer. When Israel shall be redeemed, the erstwhile shepherd can return to his flock.

Obadiah

"And Ahab called Obadiah, who was over the household. Now Obadiah feared the Lord greatly; for it was so, when Jezebel cut off the prophets of the Lord that Obadiah took a hundred prophets, and hid them fifty in a cave, and fed them with bread and water."

(1 Kings 18:3–4)

Said the Holy One, Blessed is He, "Let Obadiah, who dwelt among two wicked people, Ahab and Jezebel, but did not learn from their bad deeds, come and prophesy about Esau, who dwelt among two righteous people, Isaac and Rebecca, but did not learn from their good deeds."

(Sanhedrin 39b)

Although Obadiah was the administrator of Ahab's house, he did not feed the prophets from Ahab's wealth because Ahab had acquired his estate through thievery.

(Targum Melachim 2:4:1)

Obadiah merited prophecy because he hid one hundred prophets in a cave.

(Sanhedrin 39b)

None of the prophets could foresee what the Holy One, Blessed is He, would ultimately do to Esau, except for Obadiah the prophet, a proselyte who descended from Esau. Obadiah foresaw clearly what would befall Esau.

(Zohar 1:171a)

Obadiah, whose name means "God's servant," is credited with a single chapter book comprised of twenty-one verses. And yet this prophet of Edom (a nation associated with the inimical Esau) has already been fairly limned in the book of Kings. There he applied himself assiduously to his first career, serving as Ahab's minister of "profit." "Profit" would become "prophet" after Obadiah, recognizing the evil intention of Ahab's wife Jezebel, hid one hundred of Israel's prophets and sustained them with bread and water.

(1 Kings 18:3–4)

↗

$\mathcal{H}$e was righteous even in an evil house, and a faithful disciple of the miracle worker, Elijah. Because of his faithfulness, he was rewarded with prophecy. Familiar with evil in the service of Ahab, Obadiah's destiny was to excoriate the evil kingdom of Edom, the descendants of Esau. The rabbis view Obadiah as a descendant of Esau as well as a proselyte, and so this prophet would give an explicit vision of Esau's future.

That future was doomed. Esau would be repaid for the violence enacted against his brother Jacob. In what amounts to a pre-apocalyptic passage, Obadiah incants:

And the house of Jacob shall be a fire,
And the house of Esau for stubble,
And they shall kindle in them, and devour them;
And there shall not be any remaining of the house of Esau.
(Obadiah 1:18)

It was not an easy road, but Obadiah's career change is reminiscent of the transformation of the Israelites rendered in the *Maggid* (Narration) section of the Haggadah: "From slavery to freedom; from degradation to praise; from the kingdom of evil to the kingdom of Heaven."

Obadiah had seen evil and overcome it.

~~~

Jonah

He was equal to Elijah. Elisha anointed him.

(Mishnat Rabbi Eliezer 8)

Jonah defended the honor of the child [Israel] rather than the honor of the Father [God].

(Mechilta, Pesikta 28)

On the fifth day of the week, Jonah fled from before God's presence. Why did he flee? Jonah passed judgment upon himself. He said: "I know that this nation (the Ninevites) is close to repentance. Now they will repent, and the Holy One, Blessed is He, will vent his wrath on the Israelites who have not repented. And as if it were not enough that the Israelites call me a false prophet, even idolators will do so."

(Pirke d'Rabbi Eliezer 10)

He entered the mouth of the fish like a man entering a large synagogue, and he was able to stand up. The two eyes of the fish were like clear windows which gave light to Jonah and enabled him to see all that was in the ocean's depths. . . .

(Pirkei d'Rabbi Eliezer 10)

~~~

"*A*nd the Lord prepared a great fish to swallow up Jonah" (Jon. 2:1). This is the verse Father Mapple employs as the text of his sermon to the ill-fated shipmates of the Pequod. Father Mapple, assisted by Herman Melville, is a brilliant if fearsome expositor. He recognizes the great complexity and anguish simmering within Jonah, this most reluctant of all Israel's typically reluctant prophets. Faced with delivering a message of repentance to Israel's enemy, the Ninevites, Jonah flees instead, taking a ship to the foreign port of Tarshish.

The Lord's wishes can be abandoned, but not in the case of a prophet. The Almighty is used to recalcitrance—indeed, it seems a salient characteristic of his chosen instruments of the Word. Yet Jonah goes too far. Or does he? In a stunning midrashic re-creation of the narrative, Jonah is seen as Israel's defender, rather than as a coward who avoids his mission. This is less extraordinary than it first appears. Israel's prophets, beginning with Abraham, received righteousness "points" for coming to the aid of the nation. Defending the son against the Father was always an acceptable modus operandi in an argument with the Heavenly Court.

But first, Jonah needs time to cool off. Dunked in the ocean by his rightfully fearful co-mariners, he is swallowed, belly-up, by the underwater Leviathan for three days and three nights. The rabbis perceive the fish's enormous inner chamber as a "synagogue" in which Jonah internalizes the purpose of his mission. After he is spewed out onto dry land, he makes the pilgrimage to Nineveh. The world of Christianity perceives this tale as a symbol of the persecution and resurrection of Jesus. "The Son of man must be delivered into the hands of sinful men, and be crucified, and on the third day rise" (Luke 24:7).

Whatever one's interpretation, the meaning of the narrative is by nature parabolic. The Ninevites do repent, but Jonah, faithful to his people despite their opposition, is inconsolable. Building a *sukkah* on the east side of the city, wretched and sweltering under a relentless sun, he curses his existence. But the Lord has one more parable up His sleeve. He prepares a gourd to give Jonah shade and then causes it to wither in the heat. As Jonah writhes in misery, the Lord asks the prophet the extent of his anger. Jonah replies unhesitatingly: "I am greatly angry, even unto death." Whereupon God rejoins:

Thou hast had pity on the gourd, for which thou hast not labored, neither madest it grow, which came up in a night, and perished in a night; and should not I have pity on Nineveh, that great city, wherein are more than sixscore thousand persons that cannot discern between their right hand and their left hand, and also much cattle?

(Jon. 4:9–11)

It was a rhetorical question. But Jonah would have been wise to take it personally because, like the Ninevites, he was having considerable trouble telling his "right hand from the left."

৵

Micah

Four prophets prophesied in the same period: Hosea, Isaiah, Amos, and Micah.

(Pesachim 87a)

Six hundred thirteen precepts were told to Moses. Micah came and stressed three, as it is written: "Only to do justly, and to love mercy, and to walk humbly with thy God (Mic. 6:8).

(Makkot 24a)

Micah the Morashtite prophesied in the days of Hezekiah king of Judah, and he spoke to all the people of Judah, saying:

Zion shall be plowed as a field,
And Jerusalem shall become heaps,
And the mountain of the house as the high places of a forest.

(Jer. 26:18)

৵

*H*e lived in the late eighth and early seventh century B.C.E., a younger contemporary of Isaiah. Like an adoring disciple, Micah borrows from his master; he also extracts verses from the book of Psalms and from 2 Samuel. This inclination should not diminish his stature, for Micah must be included with Israel's most luminous prophets.

He fights for social justice, expressing particular concern for the oppression of the poor by the rich. In the process, he engages his calumnious adversaries in dialogue, revealing to the world Israel's internal conflicts with refreshing honesty and candor. Among the nations of the world Micah's frankness is unique!

Not only does Micah rehearse the same ills predicted by his worthy prophetic predecessors for Samaria and Judah, but he anticipates the birth of a shepherd king in Bethlehem (Mic. 5:1) who will restore Israel to their land and rule over them in God's name. This verse was later seized by the New Testament author Matthew (Matt. 2:6) as a prediction of the birth of Jesus.

He is a prophet of Israel but, like Isaiah, he crosses into the world of universalism. There may be no higher point in the biblical compendium than the sixth chapter of this noble prophet. What does God want? Micah suggests, the history of Israel and a host of commandments notwithstanding:

> It hath been told thee, O man what is good,
> And what the Lord doth require of thee:
> Only to do justly, and to love mercy, and to walk humbly with thy God.
>
> (Mic. 6:8)

This religious formula has been embraced and emblazoned upon the walls of many institutions of all faiths and traditions concerned with the fate of humanity.

The change is subtle, but Micah shifts from the particular interests of a nation facing devastation to the abstract subjects of love, justice, and peace. Ironic then, that the last three verses of the book (Mic. 7:18–20) are employed during the observance of *Tashlich* (the casting away of one's sins into a body of water) on the afternoon of the first day of Rosh Hashanah. This unusual custom, begun at least a millennium after Micah was written, evinces the reach of this magnificent seer of Israel, who saw everything within his world and almost as much without.

Nahum

$\mathcal{H}$e was righteous. He was also mysterious. Little is known about Nahum except that his book is a vision of the fall of Nineveh. There is also an allusion to the capture of Egyptian Thebes by Ashurbanipal in 663 B.C.E. (Nah. 3:8–10); further, there are references to the fall of Assyrian Nineveh to the Babylonians and Medes in 612. The book seems to have been composed at this precipitous time in the ancient Near East.

Nahum offers a powerful, eloquent, piercing vision of the Lord taking revenge against Israel's oppressors, the Assyrians. The language is vivid and poetic:

> She [Nineveh] is empty, and void, and waste;
> And the heart melteth, and the knees smite together,
> And convulsion is in all loins,
> And the faces of them all have gathered blackness.
>
> (Nah. 2:11)

There is a joyful sense of retaliation that accompanies these three rich prophetic chapters of the Bible. Nahum, perhaps expressing the frustration of his long-suffering people, rejoices in Nineveh's impending destruction:

> Woe to the bloody city!
> It is all full of lies and rapine;
> The prey departeth not.
> Hark! the whip, and hark! the rattling of wheels;
> And prancing horses, and bounding chariots;
> The horseman charging
> And the flashing sword, and the glittering spear;
> And a multitude of slain, and a heap of carcasses;
> And there is no end of the corpses,
> And they stumble upon their corpses.
>
> (Nah. 3:1–3)

Nahum means "comfort." What may be derived from this virile rhapsody commemorating the comeuppance of Israel's rapacious enemy is that the prophet and his people were comforted by the discomfiture of the Assyrian adversary.

Nahum, our artful mysterious poet, defender of Israel.

~

Habakkuk

Habakkuk the prophet asked the Holy One, Blessed is He: "Master of the Universe, if one person learns much and another little, will their reward be equal in the World to Come?" The Holy One, Blessed is He, replied: "No, each will be rewarded according to his ways." Since Habakkuk spoke additional words and asked why the righteous appear to be punished and the wicked appear to be rewarded, the Lord showed him all the measures of Divine justice that had been revealed to Moses, the father of wisdom and the father of prophets, who had asked a similar question. He showed him the weights and scales of Divine justice.

(*Tanna d'Bei Eliyahu Zuta* 12)

Six hundred thirteen precepts were told to Moses on Sinai. Habakkuk came and stressed one principle: "The righteous man shall live by his faith" (Hab. 2:4).

(*Makkot* 24a)

There are four who prayed and spoke harshly to the Lord out of their love for Israel: Jeremiah, Habakkuk, David, and Moses.

(*Shocher Tov* 90:2)

~

Sometimes the world can be revealed in brief. Habakkuk occupies only three chapters of the Bible, but his stirring prophecies and exalted language are reminiscent of the book of Psalms. Pathos, liturgy, disappointment, fear, anxiety—these classic themes of our suffering people are delivered by Habakkuk with a particular Jewish note of ululation.

The Chaldeans, relatives of the Arameans, are the focal point of this prophet. But beyond the specifics lies the eternal question: why, O God, does evil surmount the good? Put in a modern context: why do good things happen to bad people? Interestingly, Habakkuk posits an answer: in the end of days, the wicked will fall, but "the righteous shall live by his faith" (Hab. 2:4).

The last of Habakkuk's parables illustrates the fate of idolators:

> Woe unto him that saith to the wood: 'Awake,'
> To the dumb stone: 'Arise!'
> Can this teach?
> Behold, it is overlaid with gold and silver,
> And there is no breath at all in the midst of it.
> But the Lord is in His holy temple;
> Let all the earth keep silence before Him.
> (Hab. 2:19–20)

In exquisite contrast, Chapter 3 commences immediately with the prophet's supplications. It is a sophisticated, humble, psalm-like entreaty to the Lord in the hope of evoking both His compassion and blessing. The themes of creation, God's redemption of Israel, and His punishment of the wicked resonate throughout the succinct liturgy. Habakkuk explicates poetically the anxiety of his people in the face of such unmitigated evil, but finally, exultantly, he invokes an unshakable trust and faith in the Lord:

> God, the Lord, is my strength,
> And He maketh my feet like hinds' feet.
> And He maketh me to walk upon my high places.
> (Hab. 3:19)

Reversing the typology of the book of Psalms, Habakkuk ends his book with a formal dedication: "For the leader. With my string-music" (Hab. 3:19). As if we didn't know. Habakkuk has struck the perfect chord.

Zephaniah

An example of a righteous person who is the son of a righteous person is Zephaniah, son of Kushi.

(Megillah 15a)

"The eight princes among men" (Mic. 5:4) are Jesse, Saul, Samuel, Amos, Zephaniah, Zedekiah, Elijah, and the Messiah.

(Sukkah 52b)

He prophesied close to the destruction of the Temple.

(Seder Olam Rabbah 20)

*I*t appears he is a scion of royalty related to Hezekiah (king of Judah in the late eight century B.C.E.) and King Josiah (late seventh century B.C.E.). It was a time of upheaval—the Temple would be destroyed in 586 B.C.E.—and a time of reform, initiated by Josiah in 621. In Jerusalem, Zephaniah, whose name means "God has hidden," arises and speaks, evoking the moral concerns of his predecessors.

Indeed, Zephaniah's condemnation of Judah's failings hearkens back to the problems confronting Josiah in the book of Kings:

And I will cut off the remnant of Ba'al from this place,
And the name of the idolatrous priests with the priests;
And them that worship the host of heaven upon the housetops;
(Zeph. 1:5)

The worship of Ba'al, praying to deities of the sky, and the mimicking of their neighbors in custom and dress are old bones of contention that are dredged up by the contentious and angry prophet of the poetic soul. However, despite his anger and vituperation, Zephaniah has created an unforgettable legacy in his three-chapter prophecy.

The great day of the Lord is near,
It is near and hasteth greatly,
Even the voice of the day of the Lord,
Wherein the mighty man crieth bitterly
That day is a day of wrath,
A day of trouble and distress,
A day of wasteness and desolation,
A day of darkness and gloominess,
(Zeph. 1:14–15)

Catastrophe awaits the people, and this is no hyperbole. But those who see the light will be included in the saving remnant of Israel:

At that time will I bring you in,
And at that time will I gather you;
For I will make you to be a name and a praise
Among all the peoples of the earth,
When I turn your captivity before your eyes,
Saith the Lord.
(Zeph. 3:20)

Zephaniah is rarely mentioned when our people speak of the great prophets. Yet the rabbis knew of his righteousness. Zephaniah, our "hidden" prophet, our prince of Israel.

❧

Haggai

Haggai, Zechariah, and Malachi all prophesied in the second year of the reign of Darius.

(Megillah 15a)

Haggai, Zechariah, and Malachi received the traditions of the Torah from the prophets before them.

(Avot d'Rabbi Natan 1)

With the death of the last prophets—Haggai, Zechariah, and Malachi— Divine Inspiration departed from Israel.

(Yoma 9b)

We can place the prophetic career of Haggai with exactitude to the second year of the reign of the Persian king Darius I in 520 B.C.E. Further, Haggai tells us that his prophecy was delivered between the first of Elul and the twenty-fourth of Kislev.

(Hag. 1:1)

❧

*H*aggai is a preacher with explicit purpose. His mission was to convince the newly restored citizens of Judah to rebuild the Temple in Jerusalem. It was a new age, but the memory and admonitions of his predecessors still inform his preaching:

> Consider your ways.
> Ye have sown much, and brought in little,
> Ye drink, but ye are not filled with drink,

> Ye clothe you, but there is none warm;
> And he that earneth wages earneth wages
> For a bag with holes.
>
> (Hag. 1:5–6)

Appealing for political support from Zerubbabel, son of Judah's governor, and for religious support from Joshua, son of the High Priest, Haggai galvanizes the nation to action, cajoling and threatening his reluctant people with a discomforting thought. Unless the new Temple were erected, he said, all God's promises of salvation would come to nought.

The book is less poetic than parabolic and sermonic. As long as the Temple's restoration was ignored, the people's offerings would be rejected. The Lord wanted a refurbished home, and that would bring forth His attribute of loving kindness. For good measure, Haggai predicts the overthrow of the Persian yoke and the establishment of the kingdom of Israel:

> In that day, saith the Lord of hosts, will I take thee, O Zerubbabel,
> My servant, the son of Shealtiel, saith the Lord, and will make thee
> a signet; for I have chosen thee, saith the Lord of hosts.
>
> (Hag. 2:23)

On the twenty-fourth of Kislev, prefiguring the celebration of the Temple's rededication (Hanukkah), the foundations of the second Temple were established. It was a time of our people's religious joy. Haggai means "holiday," but life with him was certainly no picnic.

Zechariah

Zechariah is also called Meshulam (Neh. 8:4) because he was perfect in his deeds.

(Megillah 23a)

Haggai, Zechariah, and Malachi all prophesied in the second year of the reign of Darius.

(Megillah 15a)

Zechariah prophesied during the Second Temple era.

(Sanhedrin 99a)

*T*he section of the Bible in which the prophecy of Zechariah is included is known as Minor Prophets. There is nothing minor, nothing unimportant about this fourteen-chapter book, which pours forth narratives and visions whose complexity and mystery rival any section of the biblical collection.

A contemporary of Haggai, Zechariah's early prophecies may also be affixed to the reign of Darius (520–518 B.C.E.). Two sections of the book are clearly limned: chapters one through eight describe the return of Israel from the Babylonian exile; chapters nine through fourteen form an eschatological narrative. In the tradition of Haggai, Zechariah enlists support for the rebuilding of the Jerusalem Temple. Unlike Haggai, he calls forth fantastic visions that both appear and evanesce before the stunned reader.

"Stunned" is the appropriate word because if the books of the Bible are read seriatim, the type of apocalyptic images set forth in Zechariah seem way ahead of their time. Indeed, some of the prophet's depictions would find more in common with those in the New Testament's Revelations. Four horses of variegated colors standing tranquilly in the woods in the first chapter become four horns and then four craftsmen—symbolic references to the restoration of the Jerusalem Temple.

This is only the beginning. The third chapter is highlighted by a vision of the High Priest Joshua exchanging filthy garments for clean robes, and Satan, standing accusingly to his right, being rebuked by the Lord. There an angel promises Joshua that if the returning exiles obey the dictates of the Lord, they will be rewarded with "My servant the Shoot" (Zech. 3:8). This apparently is a reference to the reign of Zerubbabel, who is entrusted to rebuild the Temple.

This complex imagery receives a different reading when excerpted as the Haftarah for the Sabbath falling during Hanukkah. The reason for the association is made clear in chapter four, wherein Zechariah perceives a gold candlestick with seven lamps, accompanied by two olive trees. Having the temerity to ask the angel what this vision meant, Zechariah is rewarded with the following: "This is the word of the Lord unto Zerubbabel, saying: Not by might, nor by power, but by My spirit, saith the Lord of hosts" (Zech. 4:6).

Hanukkah is one thing. Horsemen, chariots, four winds, and oracles, another. Although scholars question whether chapters nine through fourteen belong to the first part of the narrative, there may be some justification for examining these "oracles" as part of the whole. Redemption from Babylonia is a historically verifiable period in Israel's history. Less verifiable, but just as prominent in Israel's history, is the belief that the God of our ancestors would redeem his people not only in this world but also in the next. Ezekiel moved this subject to the front burner with his popular tale of resurrection. Zechariah, whose fantastic voyage exceeds that of his literary and historical antecedents, brings the reader at least two steps closer to the world beyond the one with which we are familiar.

This includes a vision of a "triumphant king riding upon a colt, the foal of an ass" (Zech. 9:9). Why this illustration became a text for Jesus's triumphant ride into Jerusalem centuries later is clear. What may be less clear is a Jewish apocalyptic vision that has begun to wend its way into the corpus of the Bible itself. This may seem an astounding development, but it is consonant with the evolution of Jewish thought and belief and comes to a climax in the remarkable visions of Daniel.

Return, restoration, redemption. On horse, or afoot, Zechariah "saw" it all.

Malachi

"I, Daniel, alone saw the vision; but the people who were with me did not see" (Dan. 10:7). This refers to Haggai, Zechariah, and Malachi. They were superior to him in that they were prophets whom God sent to the people to deliver their prophecy whereas he was not sent to deliver any prophecy; and he was superior to them in that he saw the vision whereas they did not.

(Sanhedrin 93b)

Malachi is Mordecai. Why is he called Malachi? Because he was second to the king (*melech*) and was looked upon as an angel (*malach*) (Maharsha). However, the Talmud concludes that Malachi is Ezra.

(Megillah 15a)

His name, origin, personality, and the period in which he wrote seem to be in dispute. Based on the three chapters before us, this last of the twelve Minor Prophets is preaching his message to a people who have once again become ensconced in the Promised Land. Yes, exile is over, but apparently Israel's inclination toward evil has returned in spades.

The name of the book could well be derived from the sentence "Behold, I sent My messenger" (Mal. 3:1). "My messenger" is the translation of the Hebrew *malachi*. And this messenger has a classic prophetic message: although it is clear that the Lord loves Jacob and rejects Esau, his favored ones must recognize their obligation to serve Him with proper behavior and respect. The priestly cult, at least in this prophet's eyes, needs purification. In addition, the people must refrain from nonsanctioned behavior such as worshipping foreign gods and intermarrying.

"The messenger" is to discharge these heavenly orders. In the name of the Lord he speaks:

> But who may abide the day of his coming?
> And who shall stand when he appeareth?
> For he is like a refiner's fire.
> And like fullers' soap;
> And he shall sit as a refiner and purifier of silver,
> And he shall purify the sons of Levi,
> And purge them as gold and silver;
> And there shall be they that shall offer unto the Lord
> Offerings in righteousness.
>
> (Mal. 3:2–4).

Sanitized and purified, Judah and Jerusalem will be restored as in the days of old. More admonitions follow. The people are warned to pay their tithes wholeheartedly; failure to do so will result in exclusion from the Lord's promise of heavenly reward.

In consonance with Zechariah, whose visions explored the "end of days," Malachi adduces his own version of eschatology. That turns out to be "one hot day!"

> For, behold, the day cometh
> It burneth as a furnace;
> And all the proud, and all that work wickedness, shall be stubble;
> And the day that cometh shall set them ablaze. . . .
>
> (Mal. 3:19)

But to the God-fearers, there is hope. At last, the identity of "My messenger" is revealed. From behind the curtain emerges the mystery guest. The messenger is Elijah!

Behold, I will send you
Elijah the prophet
Before the coming
Of the great and terrible day of the Lord.
(Mal. 3:24).

Finally, Malachi invokes two ideas of smashing dissonance:

And he shall turn the heart of the fathers to the children,
And the heart of the children to their fathers;
Lest I come and smite the land with utter destruction.
(Mal. 3:24)

We end the prophetic books as they had begun. Obey God and receive the joy of victory. Disobey Him and endure the agony of defeat. At this time and in this place we are discussing nothing less than matters of eternity.

~~

Job

Job never existed; this story was only a parable.

(*Bava Batra* 15a)

No one among the nations of the world was more righteous than Job.

(*Devarim Rabbah* 2:4)

"Bless God and die" (Job 2:9). Pray before the Holy One, Blessed is He, that you should die, so that you will go from this world innocent, whole, and righteous before you come to sin; for you cannot accept the pain and you will regret your deed of the past.

(*Midrash Iyov* 14)

When suffering came upon Job, had he restrained his anger and not complained of injustice, he would have attained an extremely praiseworthy level. Just as we now say in the prayer, "God of Abraham, God of Isaac, and God of Jacob," so we would have said, "God of Job."

(*Pesikta Rabbati* 47:20)

The whole time that Job opposed his friends and his friends opposed him, the attribute of strict justice was poised. Only when he was appeased by them and prayed for them did the Holy One, Blessed is He, return to him.

(*Pesikta Rabbati* 38)

~~

*I*t begins simply, but unreasonably. Job, "a whole-hearted and upright man, one that feared God, and shunned evil" (Job 1:1), finds himself in the midst of a not-so-gentlemanly wager between God and Satan. This could be a revival of the serpent's temptation of Adam and Eve in the Garden of Eden, particularly since Job lived a life of extraordinary blessing. Yet Job was not as naive as God's first human creations. His Paradise was earned, not bestowed upon him. Knowing that evil resides in the heart of every man, Job resisted and pursued the good. The rewards of material opulence and family were kingly, if not profligate: 7,000 sheep, 3,000 camels, 500 yoke of oxen, 500 she-asses, seven sons, and three daughters.

Only the strongest of Israel were tested (see our discussion of Abraham), but the test of Job's faith is the fiercest in the Bible, the punishments unmitigating. Property, family, health—Job loses them all. And suddenly, as forlorn and lonely as he had once been happy and popular, he becomes the subject of life's greatest philosophical quest: Why do we suffer? Why does Job suffer? A midrash adduces: "Job was designated for affliction" (*Bereishit Rabbah* 30:8).

This question certainly overflowed into the New Testament, which centralizes the abandonment and suffering of mankind through the crucifixion. More pertinently, it suffuses every strand of human existence and raises existential problems. The need to understand injustice in the world—why the good seems evil and the evil good—is an age-old conundrum.

Although the book of Job has received every possible interpretation in literature (Archibald McLeish's *J.B.*, 1958, is the most noteworthy), music, and art, no answer is immediately forthcoming. Indeed, the answer can be found within Job. It is shouted, then whispered, then hidden and, finally, muted.

At first it seems that martyrdom is the best solution. Job replies to his wife, who had encouraged him to blaspheme God:

> What? shall we receive good at the hand of God, and shall we not receive evil? For all this did Job not sin with his lips.
>
> (Job 2:10)

Like any modern being, Job seeks help and counsel. Three friends come and sit with him, observing the sanctity of silence during his period of *shivah* (Job 2:11–13). It is too quiet and Job, his humanity surfacing, at last cries out:

> Let the day perish wherein I was born,
> And the night wherein it was said:
> "A man-child is brought forth."
> (Job 3:3)

Thank God for his rage, his ability to recognize his agony. His most salient characteristic has always been his patience. But to see the narrative as a paean to his fortitude is insupportable. Job is angry, and he is impatient. Chapters three through thirty-six define this part of his character, and no one, his indulgent comrades included, can deter or soften his righteous indignation. Like anybody else, he wants a reason for his suffering:

> Oh that I had one to hear me!
> Lo, here is my signature, let the Almighty answer me—
> And that I had the indictment which mine adversary hath written!
> (Job 31:35)

A fourth friend, Elihu, enters and refutes Job's denial of God. Yet it is the Almighty Himself who finally answers the loud knock on Heaven's door:

> Where wast thou when I laid the foundations of the earth?
> Declare, if thou hast the understanding.
> (Job 38:4)

This is only the beginning and an evocation of The Beginning, for the Lord invokes all creation to prove, rather obliquely, that His is the dominion, the power, and the majesty. Job meekly responds:

> Behold, I am of small account; what shall I answer Thee?
> (Job 40:4)

Yes, what is man that God takest account of him? Job knows the answer:

> Wherefore I abhor my words, and repent,
> Seeing I am dust and ashes.
> (Job 42:6)

At the end of the narrative all Job's material possessions are returned twofold. He has seven more sons and three daughters and lives another 140 years, dying "old and full of days" (Job 42:12–17). This ending, however, considered by the rabbis to be more allegorical than historical, seems out of place and not philosophically attuned to the message of the first forty-one chapters.

Job suffers. He suffers for his family. He suffers for himself. Through that suffering he attains the full reaches and depths of the human condition. It is in the appreciation of his suffering that we understand our own, internalize our own sadness and happiness, and move forward in our lives.

It is the ultimate Jewish message. Deprived, stripped bare of everything, Job speaks an eternal truth:

> Naked came I out of my mother's womb,
> And naked shall I return thither;
> The Lord gave, and the Lord hath taken away;
> Blessed be the name of the Lord.
>
> (Job 1:21)

This is our destiny, our imperative. Even amidst tragedy, we must thank and bless the Lord our God.

Ruth and Naomi

The beauty of Naomi's face put gold to shame.

(Midrash Ruth, ed. Buber, 49)

"A son is born to Naomi" (Ruth 4:17). Ruth bore him, but since Naomi raised him he was called her son.

(Sanhedrin 19b)

Whenever her mother-in-law told her, "Go, my daughter," Ruth would weep. She said, "I cannot return to my family and to the idolatrous corruption of my father's house."

(Midrash Ruth, ed. Buber, 49)

"Your people are my people, and your God is my God" (Ruth 1:16). The Holy One, Blessed is He, said to Ruth, "You have lost nothing by renouncing your birthright. Behold, the kingship is yours in this world and in the World to Come."

(Sifri Beha'alotcha 78)

Ruth the Moabitess beheld the kingdom of Solomon, her great-great grandson.

(Bava Batra 91b)

*L*ooking for a story about female bonding? Drop the patter of *Thelma and Louise* and immerse yourself in the narrative of Ruth and Naomi. This four-chapter gem qualifies as Judaism's first great short story.

The story line is simple. Because of a famine in the land of Judah, Elimelech moves his wife Naomi and two sons to Moab. There the young men take Moabite wives, Orpah and Ruth. Then (are we still connected to the book of Job?) the father and sons die, leaving three widows. Naomi wishes to return to Judah, and Ruth begs to go with her. There Ruth meets Boaz, Naomi's kinsman, who hears of Ruth's travails and betrothes her. Ruth bears a child, who is nursed by her mother-in-law. This child, Obed, is the father of Jesse, the father of King David.

Extraordinary in its simplicity, the layers of meaning are unending. That Ruth, a Moabite, one of Israel's most inimical adversaries, becomes one of the most extolled matriarchs of our people is a watershed moment in Jewish life. That she becomes the model for every present and future convert to Judaism because of her goodness and because of her purity of purpose and commitment to her mother-in-law is a great biblical milestone. That her mother-in-law Naomi (whose name means "the pleasant one") could love Ruth in return and share happiness in her daughter-in-law's life, even after she has buried a husband and two sons, becomes a paradigm for all in-law relationships.

In our time, when Jews are meeting non-Jews and seeking to share their lives together, the story provides an academic and moral lesson as well. What should be the commitment of the potential convert to Judaism? Are rules and observance the appropriate testing ground? Or love and loyalty? The book of Ruth posits the latter as Ruth clings to Naomi upon her taking leave of Moab.

Ruth says:

> Entreat me not to leave thee, and to return from following after thee; for whither thou goest, I will go; and where thou lodgest, I will lodge; thy people shall be my people, and thy God my God; where thou diest, will I die, and there will I be buried; the Lord do so to me, and more also, if aught but death part thee and me.
>
> (Ruth 1:16–17)

Yes, when the conflagration over "Who is a Jew?" is finally doused, the example of Ruth's love and loyalty to both her mother-in-law and her people will prove the validity of her Jewish transformation. It would have been perfectly acceptable if her descendants had become upstanding members of the congregation. That they became the kings of Israel and, in addition, scripted a significant part of biblical writings, was icing on the cake.

The Babylonian Talmud has handed down the tradition that in each generation there are 36 righteous people (*Lamed Vav Zaddikim*) who receive the Divine Presence (*Sanh.* 97b). Here are two of those *lamed vavniks*, the perfect pair, Ruth and Naomi.

Esther and Mordecai

There were four beautiful women: Sarah, Rahab, Abigail, and Esther.

(Megillah 15a)

Just as the myrtle (*hadas*) has a sweet smell but a bitter taste, so Esther was sweet to Mordecai but bitter to Haman.

(Esther Rabbah 6:5)

In the merit of her modesty, Rachel became the forebear of Saul; in the merit of his modesty, Saul became the forebear of Esther.

(Megillah 13b)

Mordecai in his generation was equal to Moses in his concerning the traits of humility, desiring good for his nation, and teaching of Torah to Israel.

(Esther Rabbah 6:2)

Mordecai's wife nursed Esther, and Mordecai reared her.

(Shocher Tov 22:23)

*D*avid had Jonathan, and Esther had Mordecai. These two magnificent pairs of kindred spirits faced bitter adversaries, Saul and Haman. Whereas David suffered the loss of his beloved soulmate Jonathan, Esther and Mordecai triumphed and retired as the undefeated heroes of the Jewish people.

She was an orphan, "of beautiful form and fair to look on" (Esther 1:7). Mordecai was a relative, of the house of Kish, a Benjamite, like his uncle's daughter, a descendant of King Saul. It was a precocious pairing. She employed her beauty and her ability to extemporize; he was the force behind the throne. Together they manipulated King Ahasuerus in their effort to protect their people from the hands of Haman, a descendant of Israel's most reviled enemy, Amalek. Haman had earned his evil reputation the old-fashioned way. He inherited it!

Is the story of Esther and Mordecai real or fabulistic? Centuries of Purim *shpiels* have all but done away with fair historical assessment. Yet the importance of this pair to the history of our people is unassailable, perhaps exceeding that of the recalcitrant prophet Jonah. Although many of our matriarchs were heroic, the Jew as hero is a noble paradigm. The fidelity and consonance of purpose combined with avuncular sentiment are estimable character traits.

They were a team, and as teammates they recognized the necessity of sacrificing for the cause. This was principally Esther's burden. With the Persian King Ahasuerus she played the role of ingénue; in deed she was ingenious. Emerging from sordidness, she becomes Hadassah, the sweet-smelling myrtle of Judaism, performing acts of bravery on behalf of her oppressed people.

The outcome is clear, which makes the story so palatable for children. Goodness and faithfulness triumph over treachery and evil. This is still the religious message of our people. That that message has been ignored and abused throughout history does not detract from its integrity and our need to pursue its contents wholeheartedly.

Esther and Mordecai, redeemers of Israel.

∽ᴣᴩ

Daniel

Daniel was a descendant of David.

(Zohar 3:146a)

If all the sages of the nations of the world would be on one side of the scale and Daniel, the greatly beloved man, on the other, would he not outweigh them all?

(Yoma 77a)

The Holy One, Blessed is He, revealed the coming of the Messiah to two people: Jacob and Daniel.

(Shocher Tov 31:7)

Daniel descended into the lions' pit only so that the Holy One, Blessed is He, would make wonders and miracles for him, thereby sanctifying His name in the world.

(Sifri Ha'azinu 306)

∽ᴣᴩ

*J*oseph "dreamed a dream" (Gen. 37:5) and that vision, combined with his ability to interpret the dreams of the Pharaoh, brought him success and fulfillment in the gentile world. A millennium later a new and improved Joseph emerges, initiating a different kind of Jewish thought and literature known as apocalyptic.

Intimations of this new *typos* appeared in the books of Ezekiel, Zechariah, and Malachi, but the revelations of the book of Daniel bring the reader of Scripture into a new era of Jewish/Persian/

Greek thought and a literature that hearkens to "the end of days." For a tradition that had always focused on beginnings, this approach is indeed a distinct contrast.

It is apocalyptic literature, but it straddles the old and new orders. Daniel is a brilliant Jewish youth (like Joseph) who, assuming a gentile name (Belteshazzar), goes one step further when he successfully interprets Nebuchadnezzar's dream without even being told by the Babylonian demigod what that dream was in the first place. Prophesying the rise and fall of four great monarchies (represented by an image of a head of gold, breast and arms of silver, belly and thighs of brass, legs of iron, feet of iron and clay) and a fifth monarchy (God's eternal realm), Daniel earns the king's favor and is rewarded with high office.

He is rewarded but still retains the faith of his people. Because of their rejection of the Chaldean idols and their insistence on praying to the God of Israel, Daniel and his Judean *yeshivaniks* earn a trip to the furnace and the lion's den. When they turn out to be both "fireproof" and "inedible," they are restored and promoted to higher office. It was turning out to be an arresting career.

The story of Daniel has added to the modern idiom. An idol with "clay feet" (Dan. 2), the young prophet's interpretation of the "handwriting on the wall" (Dan. 5), and Daniel in the "lion's den" (Dan. 6) are commonly employed phrases in every spoken and written language. Further, all the prophecies, dreamed and analyzed, point to the same historical results: the kingdoms of Babylon, Persia, Media, and the Greeks would perish, and the kingdom of God would triumph, both in this world and in the next.

That there is a messianic component in the narrative as well reveals the late date of this literature. This is supported by the first entrance of Aramaic into the biblical corpus, a language that began to flourish in the world of late antiquity by the third century B.C.E. Aramaic is also found in the book of Ezra. Later, the rabbis would use a slightly different form of the language, known as talmudic Aramaic, in creating their venerable compendia of the Oral Law.

He saw the new but observed the old. From Daniel the practice of praying three times a day is culled (Dan. 6:11). Also the additional liturgy of "supplication" (*Tahanun*) is derived from Chapter 9: "And I set my face unto the Lord God, to seek by prayer and supplications, with fasting, and sackcloth, and ashes" (verse 3).

Daniel, our new Joseph, our prophet, our liturgist.

Ezra and Nehemiah

When Torah was forgotten by Israel, Ezra came up from Babylon and reestablished it.

(Sukkah 20a)

Ezra did not ascend from Babylon until he had recorded his genealogy. He wrote his book and the genealogy of Chronicles until he reached the genealogy of himself. Who finished it? Nehemiah, son of Hacaliah.

(Bava Batra 15a)

Nehemiah spent twelve years in the land of Israel fixing the walls of Jerusalem and returning the people of Israel, each one to his city and to his inheritance.

(Seder Olam Rabbah 30)

*A*fter the apocalyptic vision of Daniel, one might be surprised by the contents of Ezra and Nehemiah. Part of Ezra is written in Aramaic, indicating a late fifth- or early fourth-century B.C.E. origin. The thrust of the book is historical and legal rather than revelatory. Scholars suggest that the books of Ezra and Nehemiah were originally a single composition since the latter includes the deeds of the former.

Nearly a century after the Persian king Cyrus issued an edict allowing the Jews to return to Israel and rebuild the Temple, Ezra

and Nehemiah assume positions of leadership in the congregation of Israel. Ezra is the scribe who proffers the words of the law;
Nehemiah is the governor who makes sure the rebuilding of
Jerusalem meets his specifications. Ezra makes a late appearance
in his own book. Nevertheless, his mission is clearly delineated:
"For Ezra had set his heart to seek the law of the Lord, and to do
it, and to teach in Israel statutes and ordinances" (Ezra 7:10). This
resolution, in addition to Artaxerxes's royal stamp of approval,
concretizes his assignment.

Nehemiah responds out of sympathy for Jerusalem's plight. His
political acumen, both in his position as cupbearer with Artaxerxes
and later as governor of Judah, secures and exalts his position.
What follows is a remarkable series of repairs in the land. Gates,
doors, walls, houses, and cities receive Nehemiah's complete attention as well as second coats of paint.

Yet the great religious moment belongs to Ezra who "on the
first day of the seventh month" reads the law of Moses in front
of the wayward flock. Nehemiah supports Ezra's efforts in a
jointly issued statement to the children of Israel: "This day is
holy unto the Lord your God; mourn not, nor weep. . . . Go your
way, eat the fat, and drink the sweet, and send portions unto
him for whom nothing is prepared; for this day is holy unto our
Lord; neither be ye grieved; for the joy of the Lord is your
strength" (Neh. 8:9–11).

It may be accidental, but as we ponder and consider the multitude of biblical personalities who presided over the spiritual and
physical evolution of our people, we might note how the
penultimate verses of Scripture support and confirm the Five
Books of Moses. The Prophets ushered in a new period of Jewish
thought and practice but, despite this transformation, the biblical imprimatur endures: "Ye shall be holy; for I the Lord your God
am holy" (Lev. 19:2).

Ezra and Nehemiah. Scribe and governor. Restorers of Jerusalem and the Law.

Index

ABOUT THE AUTHOR

Rabbi Richard S. Chapin has served Congregation Emanu-El of New York since 1979. He was ordained from Hebrew Union College in 1976 and earned his D.H.L. in 1990. He graduated from Hamilton College in 1971. He has taught courses in the New Testament at New York University and in Biblical Hebrew at the Dalton School. His scholarship has focused on the period of Late Antiquity and the meeting of the Jewish and Christian "schools" in the Syrian Orient. His rabbinate has involved him in all stages of the Jewish life cycle—with particular emphasis upon the Jewish education of young children and the teaching of American-Jewish literature to adults. He lives in Yonkers with his son, Joshua.